SYSTEMS ANALYSIS IN POLITICAL SCIENCE

SYSTEMS ANALYSIS IN POLITICAL SCIENCE

A Marxist Critique of David Easton

Dr. A.K. Baruah
Political Science of Department
North-Eastern Hill University
Shillong-793014 (Mizoram)

UPPAL PUBLISHING HOUSE
NEW DELHI - 110002

UPPAL PUBLISHING HOUSE
3, Ansari Road, Daryaganj, New Delhi-110002

ISBN 81-85024-25-1

PRINTED IN INDIA
Published by B.S. Uppal, UPPAL PUBLISHING HOUSE, 3, Ansari Road, Daryaganj, New Delhi-110002, and Printed at Latika Printers, Old Maujpur, Shahdara, Delhi-110053.

Preface

In the field of contemporary political, theary, Professor David Easton occupies a very prominent place. During a period when political theory, as a field of study, was, by and large, ignored, he argued strongly in its favour and tried to build a theory of his own which he calls a conceptual framework. While some scholars have praised his framework sky high others have called it a futile exercise. But, despite the interest and the controversies generated by Easton's writings, no systematic attempt has so far been made to study his ideas in their totality. This book is an attempt in that direction. It is necessary for such a work to take into account all the writings of Easton and also to keep tract of the latest developments in his thought. Professor Easton very kindly supplied me some of his publications which are not easily available. In one of his visits to India, he talked to me in great details about some crucial issues. These discussions with him are added to this book, as an interview, in the appendix. I wish to record my thanks to Professor Easton for the help and cooperation I received from him. My special thanks go also to Professor Shanti Swarup, who supervised my Ph. D. work on Easton. Had it not been for the long discussions and the constant guidance I received from him, thisbook would have been impossible. I have also benifited greatly from my discussions, with Professors S. P. Verma, Iqbal Narain, K. Sheshadri, and Krishna Bharadwaj, on systems analysis. Professor C.P. Bhambhri read an earlier draft and made valuable comments. I take this opportunity to thank my friends Mr. Pritam Singh Gill, and Dr. S.P. Gautam of the Panjab University and Dr. Pramod Kumar of CRRID, Chandigarh for their valuable suggestions. My wife Ms. Manorama Sharma of Gauhati University prepared the transcript of my recorded interview with Easton. I must also acknowledge that my discussions with her on many aspects of this work have always proved highly fruitful.

I am grateful to the editor of the *Punjab Journal of Politics* for allowing me to reproduce my article "American Political Science and the Study of Theory" from his journal.

North-Eastern Hill University,
Shillong—793014 (Mizoram).

Apurba Kumar Baruah

Contents

CHAPTER 1

Introduction

In the fifties of this century American political science came fully under the influence of behaviouralism, which emphasised the study of facts. Despite the resistance from traditional political science, the behaviouralists came to dominate the discipline in such a manner that the whole discipline became engrossed in factual research. This obsession with factual research led to a neglect of the study of political theory.

The behavioural conquest of American political science, thus, created a situation where theoretical inquiry came to be regarded as a suspicious, unsatisfactory, and perhaps illogical form of thought.[1] It is remarkable that during the same period a group of political scientists began to express concern over the decline of political theory. Peter Laslett and Rober A. Dahl declared that political theory was "dead".[2] Neal

1. This point has been argued repeatedly by Political Scientists. However, for an exposition of the impact of behaviouralism on study of political theory in America see, Ithiel de Solapool, (ed.) *Contemporary Political Science : Toward Empirical Theory*, (New York, 1967) ; Rosemean, Mayo, and Collinge, *Dimensions of Political Analysis*, (New Jersey, 1965).

2. See Peter Laslett, (ed.) *Philosophy, Politics and Society*, first series (New York, 1957) ; Robert A. Dahl, "Political Theory" *World Politics*, Vol. XI (October 1958), pp.89-102.

Reimer said that political theory was "in the dog house".[3] Alfred Cobban and David Easton wrote about its "decline".[4] Scholars may have differed about the nature and causes of this decline; but a majority of political scientists with the exception of a few like Dante Germino[5] agreed that there was a decline in the study of political theory. Randhir Singh rightly said that though there had been differences of opinion about diagnosis and remedies yet there was a consensus about the existence of a situation of real trouble.[6]

Among these authors who tried to draw the attention of the discipline to the decline of political theory, Professor David Easton was, probably the most important. He had not only pointed out the decline of political theory but also ventured "to win back for theory its proper and necessary place."[7] Though Easton begins by refering to the decline of political theory in general, he is particularly disturbed about the state of political theory in the United States. His comments on the state of political theory in America, however, becomes a commentary on the state of political theory in general because political science in its present form is almost

3. See Neal Reimer, *The Revival of Democratic Theory*, (New York, 1962), p. 1.
4. Alfred Cobban, *In Search of Humanity,* (New York, 1960) pp. 20-29, 229-245 and "The Decline of Political Theory" *Political Science Quarterly*, Vol. LXVIII (September, 1953), pp. 321-337 ; David Easton. *The Political System : An Enquiry into the State of Political Science* (New York, 1953), Chapter 10, and "The Decline of Modern Political Theory" in James A. Gould and Vincent V. Thursby, (eds) *Contemporary Political Thought* (New York, 1969), pp. 307-27.
5. Danto Germino argues that during the period in which the above mentioned scholars and a host of others were speaking of a decline of political theory it was actually reviving. See Dante Germino, "The Revival of Political Theory" *The Journal of Politics*, Vol. 2 (August 1963), pp. 437-460. See also his book *Beyond Ideology : The Revival of Political Theory*, (New York, 1967).
6. Randhir Singh, *Reason Revolution and Political Theory*, (New Delhi, 1976), p. 8, fn. 12.
7. Easton, *The Political System, op. cit.*, p. XV.

entirely an American discipline.[8] In the opening paragraph of *The Political System*, Easton says :

> ... in the light of what society demands from them and of what is in fact possible for political science, they (political scientists) would be compelled... to set all pride aside and confess that in its achievement in research American political science has great difficulty in measuring up to the task imposed upon it.[9]

He then states the reason for this failure in the following words :

> It is the burden of this study that among these reasons and at the fore front we must place the constant reluctance in American political science to adopt and teach seriously the standards of valid thinking, observation and description which today we are prone to associate with something vaguely called scientific method.[10]

Easton rightly argues that acceptance, and introduction into ongoing research, of the fundamental postulates and assumptions of this method would reveal that "a major source of the shortcomings in political science lies in the failure to clarify the true relationship between facts and political theory and the vital role of theory in this partnership."[11] This failure of course has its roots in the very history of political

8. Gabriel Almond says, "...although political philosophy and political analysis are ancient fields of inquiry—primarily Mediterranean and European in their origin—political science as a profession with specialisation of interests, substantial research support, emphasis on systematic field research, and rigorous logical methods, is relatively new and at the present time is almost entirely American." Gabriel Almond, "Political Theory and Political Science", in Ithiel de Solapool, *op. cit.*, p. 4.

9. Easton, *op. cit.*, p. 3.

10. *Ibid.*, pp. 3-4.

11. *Ibid.*, p. 4.

enquiry. Eversince the days of Plato traditional political science has engaged itself mainly in the construction of Utopian systems, i.e., ideal States and societies. The concern with the ideal made traditional political science a normative exercise. In the process the study of facts, very often, remained neglected. Emergence of behaviouralism led to a break in this tradition. The early behaviouralists emphasized the study of facts. As a result traditional political science came to face severe criticism. But the point to be noted here is that while most of the traditional political scientists indulged in purely normative theorizing at the cost of factual research the early behaviouralists concentrated on facts at the cost of theory.

A rigorous scientific method should help us to restore theory to its proper place because a fundamental requirement of any science is that facts and theories must be inter-related so that theories attempt to explain facts and facts help generate or test new theories. New factual data may change or destroy theories. It can also generate new theories, which, in turn, may alter the basis and pattern of the collection and analysis of data.[12] Easton holds that the search for reliable knowledge about empirical phenomena requires ultimately the construction of systematic theory, the name for the highest order of generalization.[13] He maintains that American political science failed to develop such a theory because it fell a prey to, what Easton calls, 'Hyper-factualism'.[14] This overemphasis on "facts" in scientific research pushed theoretical perspective to the background. Moreover, political scientists were reluctant to separate pure science from what is variously called practical, prescriptive, or applied science. As a result

12. For a discussion on this point see Robert Dublin, *Theory Building*, (New York, 1969); p. 7 and Arnold Brecht, *Political Theory : The Foundations of Twentieth Century Political Thought*, (Bombay, 1965), pp. 17-21.

13. Easton, *op. cit.*; p. 4.

14. *Ibid.*, pp. 66-78.

political scientists attempted to build 'a premature policy science'[15] Easton concludes :

> ... Over the years political science has emerged as a fact gathering and reforming discipline. While verification of theory obviously requires the accumulation of facts and social reality demands the application of knowledge, nevertheless excessive emphasis on these aspects of research has both reflected and contributed to the concealment of the necessary theoretical foundation for any mature understanding of the political system. In concentrating on the accumulation of facts, political science has neglected the general framework within which these facts could acquire meaning to transcend any particular time and place And in becoming pre-occupied almost exclusively with problems of applying this factual information, political science has impeded its own movement towards a fundamental understanding of political life, a kind of knowledge that would place the relation of means to ends on a secure foundation.[16]

As is evident from the above passage, though Easton arrives at these conclusions on the basis of his observation of the condition of the American political science his plea for developing a theory in the form of a 'general framework' is meant for the discipline as a whole. All through his book *The Political System* Easton emphasizes the need for a political theory in the form of a general framework of analysis which may enable us to order "all" political data.

Though this clearly is a plea for an empirical theory of politics Easton does not ignore the questions of values. He argues that moral views influence theoretical thinking to such a degree that a conceptual framework would be incomplete without a clear knowledge and understanding of its moral premises. Secondly, that mere description of formal

15. *Ibid.*, p. 78.
16. *Ibid.*, p. 89.

knowledge of these ethical premises does not meet this requirement for moral clarity. Thirdly, that the need for closer attention to systematic theory automatically imposes upon political science the obligation to re-examine and ultimately to revise the way in which moral theory has been studied over the first half of the twentieth century.[17] Easton shows that the approaches of authors like Dunning, Mcllwain and Sabine to the study of political theory resulted in a "decline into historicism".[18] He maintains that these political theorists are primarily historicist in their orientation. They do not use the history of values as a device to stimulate thought on a possible constructive redefinition on political goals".[19] Easton wants political scientists to take a constructive approach to the question of value judgement. Such an approach must enable them to clarify their moral premises and to detect the influence of moral views on their research in systematic theory.[20]

Any attempt at formulating such a theory immediately necessitates a definition of politics on the basis of which political phenomena could be distinguished from other social phenomena. Easton reviews all prevailing definitions of politics and finds that these centre round the concepts of state and power. The inadequacies of these concepts[21] compel him to offer a new definition of politics. He defines politics as "authoritative allocation of values for a society".[22] This definition as Frohock says, is "perhaps the most widely known modern definition of political phenomena"[23]. Frohock has pointed out the obvious advantages of the definition.

17. *Ibid.*, pp. 219-232.
18. *Ibid.*, pp. 233-265.
19. *Ibid.*, p. 253.
20. *Ibid.*, p. 265.
21. *Ibid.*, pp. 91-124.
22. Ibid., p. 129.
23. Fred, M. Frohock, *The Nature of Political Inquiry* (Homewood Illinois, 1967), p. 88.

These are: it focuses on activity instead of institutions, it escapes the definitional morass of power and it provides a general framework for locating political variables.[24] But, this definition has not been universally accepted. Frohock himself maintains that since under this definition only authoritative allocations could be regarded as political phenomena, "to remain consistent, we must exclude a number of policy decisions made by governments which do not quite fit the proposal".[25] He argues that many decisions of legally constituted officials are not allocative in nature. Moreover, Easton's definition regards only those policies as authoritative which are considered binding by the people for whom they are made. In that sense gevernment policies and decisions which are not implemented will not be considered political. Evans shows that the key terms in the definition are ambiguous and therefore it fails to define political phenomena.[26]

However, on the basis of this definition Easton develops a framework for political analysis. He argues that political life is an activity and it must be viewed as a system. His idea of the political system has evoked great interest among political scientists. Meehan has lauded it as "one of the few comprehensive attempts to lay the foundation for systems analysis in political science and provide a 'general' functional theory of political science".[27] Oran Young calls it "undoubtedly the most inclusive systemic approach so far constructed specifically for political analysis by a political scientist". As this is an approach developed specially for political science Young sees in it the advantage of being "able to deal with the various problems of applying systems

24. *Ibid.*, p. 89.

25 *Loc. cit.*

26. Michael Evans "Notes on David Easton's Model of the Political System" *Journal Commonwealth Studies*, Vol. 8, (July 1970), pp. 124-129.

27. Eugene Meehan, *Contemporary Political Thought* (Illinois, 1967), p. 169.

analysis to political questions in a coordinated fashion without having to cope with problems of adaptation".[28] Easton's model is not universally acclaimed. Some political scientists have pointed out defects in the model. Others have even questioned the utility of his whole exercise. Paul F. Kress for instance says that it may best be described as an "empty vision" of politics. He writes, "by the phrase 'empty vision', I wish to summarize my arguments concerning the theory's lack of substance, the artificial nature of system and member, the replacement of the action by the container, and the disappearance of boundaries as limits of possibility".[29] Another critic Thomas Landon Thorson argues that Easton's framework is based on the prediction-generalization model of science and that Easton aims at building an all-time, all-space general theory of politics. He maintains that such a theory is not possible. Thorson writes:

> Easton really performs a considerable service for students of politics although certainly not the one he intended to perform.... By showing us that a political system, construed in an absolutely general way, fails to persist only in those cases where it fails to persist Easton convinces us ....that the enterprise is futile.[30]

Such differences of opinion about Easton's ideas are the results of some what piecemeal studies of his works. Studies which have discussed Easton's ideas on political theory, definition of politics and the conceptual framework developed by him separately have neither examined systematically the inter-connections between these nor have they traced the evolution of Easton's thought. In fact despite the interest aroused by his writings no systematic attempt has so far been

28. Orang Young, *Systems of Political Science* (New Jersey, 1968), p. 46.
29. Paul F. Kress "A Critique of Easton's Systems Analysis", in James A. Gould and Vincent Thursby, *op. cit.*, p. 226.
30. Thomas Landon Thorson, *Bio-Politics,* (New York, 1970), pp. 70-71.

made to study Easton's ideas in their totality. This study is an attempt at this direction.

David Easton has concerned himself with the decline of modern political theory, particularly in American political science. He has argued the importance of political theory in the study of politics. He gives a new definition of politics and on the basis of this definition develops a 'general theory of politics' in the form of a conceptual framework which he calls a systems analysis of political life. With the help of this framework he also takes up some empirical studies in the area of political socialization. Therefore, an assessment of Easton's contribution must consider each of these areas of his research. Such an assessment is possible only if we begin by examining his idea of political science as a discipline, its nature and scope. Easton, as we have pointed out writes as an American political scientist and it is only natural that his perception of the nature and scope of the discipline would to a great extent be influenced by the nature of the American political science itself. Any attempt at understanding this nature would necessitate an analysis of the history of the emergence of American political science and the intellectual milieu, social environment and the forces that gave shape to this history. It is in this context that Easton's arguments about the importance of political theory, the nature of his theory, the definition of politics and his empirical work in the field of political socialization must be understood. Such a study of course cannot ignore the process of evolution of his thought; because an analysis of the evolution of his ideas would reveal the various phases of his thought and would enable us to understand the main sources of influence that shape these phases.

Easton's main concern is political theory. It is this concern that pervades his writings. A political theory is a means for understanding a political reality. To assist understanding it has to clarify; and to clarify it has to simplify. A political theory then must be based on a simplification of the political reality; which in itself is a notion of reality. Such a notion comprises of hypotheses about reality. These hypotheses amount to tentative suggestions about reality and therefore involve a conceptualized view of the reality. A reality can be viewed either as static or as dynamic. A perspective from which a reality is viewed becomes a perspective for the analysis of the reality itself. As Allen puts it:

> A conceptualization of reality as static implies that it has qualities which make for consensus which gave it an organic unity, which are prior to any other qualities. A conceptualization of reality as a changing phenomenon gives priority to qualities which produce change.[31]

A theory which is based on a view of society which is static will be a theory which is status-quoist in nature and a theory which is based on a dynamic view of society will be free from such a bias. Therefore, while trying to understand Easton's political theory, the two major questions we plan to raise are : 1) Does his political theory help us to simplify political reality so that we can understand it? 2) Does he view reality as static or as changing?

To facilitate our inquiry in this direction we have divided the study into seven chapters. The first chapter traces the emergence and development of American political science and its treatment of political theory. The second chapter evaluates Easton's ideas on the nature of political theory against the background of the development of political theory in America. Since his views on political theory are closely connected with his definition of politics so the third chapter analyses this definition. Fourth and the fifth chapters analyse the viability of Easton's framework and the question of maintenance and persistence in his framework. Sixth chapter is a discussion of Easton's work in the area of political socialization. The last chapter summarises the discussion and attempts to arrive at some conclusions.

31. V.L. Allen, *Social Analysis : A Marxist Alternative* (London, 1975), p. 16.

CHAPTER 2

Neglect of Political Theory and American Political Science

Neglect of political theory in the American political science is not a recent phenomenon. All through its history, American political science has either neglected political theory or handled it in a manner that hampered its growth. To comprehend this trend, one must analyse the socio-political atmosphere in which American political science emerged and developed as a discipline.

The emergence of American political science can be traced back to the later half of the nineteenth century. To be precise, it was only in 1880 that John W Burgess succeeded in establishing a separate school of political science at the columbia university. This is not to suggest that prior to this event political matters were not studied at all in America. Upto 1880, courses in Philosophy, moral philosophy and ethics used to include some political matters; but there was no integrated course in political science.[1] Bernard Crick observes that until after the civil war political science scarcely existed as a

1. For a detailed discussion on the teaching of political science in America from 1636-1900 see Hanna Haddow, *Political Science in American Colleges and Universities from 1636-1900* (New York, 1936).

subject in the teaching of American colleges.[2] But over the years, the study of politics grew in size as well as in status and by the eighth decade of the nineteenth century it began to emerge as a discipline.

Reconstruction reform and pragmatism

These years of emergence of political science were the years following the civil war. The American society, in these years, was undergoing a phase of reconstruction. It was facing a series of crucial problems. As Nye and Morpurgo put it :

> The Southerner's problem was three fold : to adjust to a new set of social and economic conditions; recreate a new political society; and pick up the pieces (if he could) of a life shattered by war. The north meanwhile was concerned with consolidating victory, retaining control of the federal government, and establishing economic and political authority over the conquered confederacy.[3]

It was only natural that in a period of such drastic changes and reconstruction, the dominant section of the American society wanted to train its citizens to accept the new order and the values attached to it. As is evident from our discussion below, of the nature and scope of the American political science during that period, this emerging discipline came to their help.

In the early stage of its growth political science was making use of political writings like The Declaration of Independence and the Constitution, the Federalist papers, Presidential addresses, State Papers, Texts of Judicial decision, famous speeches of statesmen and important editorials of newspapers and journals. All these formed the materials for the students

2. Bernard Crick, *American Science of Politics* (Berkley and Los Angels, 1959), p. 12.
3. R.B. Nye and J.E. Morpurgo, *A History of the United States: The Growth of the United States : The Growth of the USA*, Vol. 2, (Hammondsworth, 1965), p. 53.

of political science. This material was conducive to what Crick calls "the inaugural purpose of the American Political Science". Crick identifies this purpose as training people to become good citizens and training youngmen for public service.[4] The discipline remained engrossed in these programmes of training and neglected the study of theory.

In the beginning of the twentieth century, American Political Science took a new turn. In this period American Society was undergoing a series of reforms. The general state of affairs were such that liberal thinkers became utterly dissatisfied with their crisis ridden society. To some of them the federal government appeared to be controlled by a privileged few who ran it for the benefit of the rail roads, the banks and the manufacturing and mining corporations.[5] This was the time when millions of men found themselves unemployed, who could not make a living. The liberal thinkers of this period, disturbed by the situation, held that there was something wrong with the system.[6] What followed was a current of a reformism in political thinking which was known as progressivism as well as populism. Civil Service reform, the direct election of Senators, electoral reforms, the reconstruction of municipal government, the initiative and referendum were the main themes of progressivism and populism. Since these trends dominated the American Society; it was no wonder that political science of this period was caught in these currents. The main themes of progressivism and populism became a part of the political science of the time.[7] These issues engrossed the discipline so much that theoretical issues remained by and large neglected.

4. Crick, *op. cit*, pp. 21-31.
5. Nye and Morpurgo, *op. cit.*, p. 606.
6. J.D. Hicks : "The populist contribution", in Donald Spechan (ed.) *The Making of American History*, (New York, 1954), p. 707.
7. See Dwight Waldo, "Political Science, : Tradition, Discipline Profession, Science, Enterprise" in Fred I. Greenstein and Nelson W Polsby (ed.) *Handbook of Political Science*, Vol. I. (Reading, 1975) p. 39.

Neglect of political theory during this era had a philosophical basis too. Pragmatism, the dominant philosophy of the period emphasised 'practical consequences' and thus created an intellectual milieu in which theory remained neglected. The extent to which this philosophy influenced all the social sciences could be understood from the fact that, by the early twenties there was scarcely a social scientist who did not consider himself to be in some sense, a pragmatist. "To follow the pragmatic method", says Landau, "meant to look at social life as it really was, to attend to social institutions as they *really looked*, to find the *how* of things not the why". (emphasis in original).[8] To be a pragmatic is to rely not upon laws, rules, and principles but upon makeshifts, rule of thumb methods, and impoverisations based on what is believed to be immediately advantageous.[9]

William James and Charles Sanders Pierce were the real founders of American Philosophic Pragmatism. Pragmatism is distinguished by its trial and error approach. James, for instance, says :

> The pragmatic method is primarily a method of settling metaphysical disputes that otherwise might be interminable. Is the world one or many ? fated or free? material or spiritual?—here are notions either of which may or may not hold good of the world; and disputes over such notions are unending. The pragmatic method in such cases is to try to interpret each notion by tracing its respective practical consequences.[10]

If pragmatism is a method of settling disputes by tracing their practical consequences then it is possible for it to overlook the moral and ideological implications of the issues

8. Martin Landau : *Political Theory and Political Science,* (New York, 1972), pp. 128-129.

9. George Novack, *Pragmatism versus Marxism* (New York, 1975), p. 17.

10. William James, *Pragmatism* (New Delhi, 1975), p. 42.

involved in such disputes. This aspect of pragmatism is reflected clearly in the approach of the most influencial American pragmatist John Dewey. His approach, instrumentalism, emphasises the practical consequences of issues and events. Elliott rightly says that instrumentalism does not look to an evaluation of moral ends but takes these ends for granted as the datum of the social situation of every act. These acts are to be tested only in terms of their efficiency in attaining the given ends.[11]

Though pragmatism was a philosophy and had implications for moral philosophy, at the methodological level it did emphasize practical consequences. This emphasis made pragmatism refer to the usefulness, workability, and practicality of ideas policies, and proposals as criteria of their merit and claims to attention. Pragmatism welcomed change and explained how to direct it intelligently. It supplied a general tool for the reformist thought of the progressive era. Like other social sciences political science also came under the influence of this philosophy.

The influence of Reformism and Pragmatism made citizenship training the 'raison d' etre' of political science. As a result political science in the United States acquired an essentially practical character, in a narrow sense. It came to limit itself to the study of immediate problems which in turn stripped it of any long term perspective. It is only natural that a science motivated basically by such ideas would neglect theoretical thinking. This, of course, should not create the impression that during this period there was no theoretical work at all. There, indeed, was a political scientist like A.F. Bently who paid considerable attention to the problems of a theoretical nature. Bently published his *The Process of Government* in 1908.[12] He rejected all metaphy-

11. W.Y. Elliott, *Pragmatic Revolt in Politics*, (New York, 1928), p. 224.

12. A.F. Bently : *The Process of Government*, (Bloomington 1949). This book was first published in 1908.

sics and normative formulations. He criticized the barren formalism of the political science of his time and said that even a dose of metaphysics could not save such studies.[13] Bently insisted that the proper study of politics was that of observable facts. Facts, according to Bently, must be studied in the context of the "group". He used the 'group' as the basic concept. The analysis of these groups was considered to be the main task in the study of any form of social life. He wrote, "when the groups are adequately stated, everything is stated".[14] He was of the opinion that if we could get our social life in terms of activity and nothing else, we had not indeed succeeded in measuring it, but we had at least reached a foundation upon which a coherent system of measurement could be built up.[15] His approach does not neglect political theory totally, because the problem which Bently tried to tackle was itself a theoretical one. With the help of the concept of group he tried to explain the process of government as one in which the social policy is decided upon as a result of "push and resistance between groups".[16] Merriam and Barnes said in 1924 that *The Process of Government* was regarded by many penetrating critics as the most notable American contribution to political theory.[17] But in spite of the theoretical implications of his ideas the work of Bently remained by and large ignored by the political scientists of his time. Easton writes, "It is true that until recently Bently's work has had no discernible influence on the growth of American political science; reference to it does not begin until the twenties with the rise of interest group politics."[18] Bernard Crick has also pointed out that for a long time Bently's influence remained obscure.[19]

13. *Ibid.*, p. 162.
14. *Ibid.*, p. 208.
15. *Ibid.*, p. 202.
16. Ibid., p. 258.
17. Charles E Merriam, Hanry, E. Barnes, (ed.), *A History of Political Theories in Recent Times : Essays in Contemporary Developments in Political Theory* (New York, 1924), p. 363.
18. Easton, *op. cit.*, p. 176.
19. Crick, *op. cit.*, p. 119.

Thus, except for the isolated and ignored attempt of Bently American Political Science, during its formative period, neglected the study of political theory. In a period of major change and reconstruction the discipline remained engrossed in the problems of reform and citizenship training.

The spell of Scientism

In the inter-war period American political science came under the influence of Scientific method. Between the two wars the socio-political situation in America became rather complicated and the dominant section of the American society began to feel insecure. As Oscar Handlin puts it :

> Although disaster did not come, there was a basic to the fear of respectable Americans. Social conditions were deteriorating to a point at which it was no longer safe to take the docility of the population for granted. Deepening class divisions were bringing the united states close to the tense revolutionary situation of the Europeans.[20]

The dominant section of the American society wanted to avoid a major social upheaval. In their bid to save the situation they adopted a pragmatic approach to politics. "The point of politics...was to understand the actual operation of government, to study unwritten as well as written laws, to recognize the political importance of men and pressures and opinions".[21] There is a very strong conservative bias in this approach. If one studies only what in fact and actually happens one does not raise normative questions about the just or unjust nature of the system. Instead of looking at the normative aspect of the issues involved American political scientists of that period tried to build a scientific method for the study of politics. This of course was understandable because to the early twentieth century 'science'

20. Oscar Handlin, *America : A History* (New York, 1968) p. 703.

21. Nye and Morpurgo, *op. cit.*; p. 588.

appeared to be the magic word the key to the solution of all problems.

Early twentieth century was an era of scientific progress. The basis of this progress was the descriptive work of the Nineteenth Century. A series of discoveries and inventions in the fields of physics, chemistry and medicine took place in this period. It seemed that the triumphs of science would bring knowledge and power in abundance. As a result prestige of science increased enormously and the effectiveness of the methods of science became almost an established fact. There is no wonder that social scientists, including political scientists, were enamoured by the scientific method.

By this time disciplines like Anthropology, Sociology and Psychology began to rise. Economics was already a discipline of status and recognition.[22] Political scientists could not ignore the fact that these disciplines were using methods which were considered more scientific. In their bid to be scientific they tried to build a science of politics on the lines of these disciplines.

Charles E. Merriam was one of the pioneers in this field. Fascinated by the achievements of science he took a very critical view of political science of his time for its lack of scientific rigour and urged political scientists to use scientific methods to study the important forces of political and social control. He, in fact, felt that if political scientists failed to use scientific methods there would be a jungle of politics. He wrote :

> What advantages shall we reap if science conquered the whole world except the world's government and then turns its titanic forces over to a government of ignorance and

22. For a discussion of the development of various Social Science disciplines in the U.S.A., see, L.L. Bernard "Political Science" in Edwin R.A. Seligman, (ed) *Encyclopedia of Social Sciences*, vol. II (New York, 1967), pp. 324-349.

prejudice, with laboratory science in the hands of jungle governors?[23]

Merriam hoped that science would help the political scientists to liberate government from the hold of ignorance and prejudice.

These ideas were not entirely new. We have already mentioned that psychology had already established itself as a 'Scientific' discipline. Some students of political life argued for application of scientific method in political science on the basis of their understanding of this method in psychology. As early as 1908 Grahma Wallas wrote that modern psychology offered a conception of human nature much truer, though complex than that which was associated with the traditional English political philosophy; and that under the influence and example of the natural sciences, political thinkers were already beginning to use in their discussions and enquiries quantitative rather than merely qualitative words and methods, and were able, both to state their problem more fully and to answer them with a greater approximation to accuracy.[24] Wallas, wanted political scientists to emulate the psychologists in the adoption of scientific method. He argued that a political science should be based upon quantitative methods and that serious attention should be paid to the psychological elements in political activity, including non-rational acts and the exploitation in political life of sub-conscious and non-rational inferences.

Similar views were expressed by Walter Lippman who emphasized the importance of psychological elements in political activity. He argued that the state craft must take human nature as its basis but must not use self introspection as a tool of psychological analysis. The method of introspec-

23. Charles, E. Merriam, *New Aspects of Politics* (Chicago, 1925), p. 11.

24. Graham Wallas, *Human Nature in Politics,* (Bombay, 1948, Originally published in 1908), p. 167.

tion, he maintained was based on the assumption that the only experience we really understand is our own.[25] He argued that experience had enlarged our knowledge of differences. We realized now that our neighbour was not always like ourselves. Knowing how unjust other people's inferences were when they concern us, we had begun to guess that ours might be unjust to them.[26] Lippman, therefore, emphasised the role of observable psychological data in the study of politics.

Almost all the issues that Merriam raised about the scientific method in political science could be traced back to the writings of Lippman. Like Merriam, Lippman also held that statistical method would be helpful for political research. He emphasised the necessity of practical research and urged political scientists to direct their attention to practical politics.[27] He wanted political scientists to do all this on the basis of facts because he was a great believer in the authority of facts as against reason. But to be really accurate Lippman was more concerned with technical skill rather than scientific method. This becomes clear from his views about the role of the social scientists. He argued that every complicated community had sought the assistance of specialized men. The Statesmen, the executive, the party leader, the head of a voluntary association had found that if he had to discuss two dozen different subjects in the course of the day somebody would have to coach him.[28] Lippman pointed out, "Yet curiously enough, though he knew that he needed help, he was slow to call in the social scientists."[29]

In the hands of Merriam the same ideas became parts of a passionate argument for the development of a scientific

25. Walter Lippman, *A Preface to Politics*, (Ann. Arbor, 1962), p. 85.
26. *Loc. cit.*
27. *Ibid.*, pp. 71-72.
28. Walter Lippman, *Public Opinion*, (New York, 1947), pp. 69-71.
29. *Ibid.*, p. 71.

method The trend set by Merriam continued and in fact got strengthened with the publication of a series of books which emphasized the need for a scientific method in the study of politics. G.E.C. Catlin published *Science and Methods in Politics* in 1927.[30] Stuart, A. Rice made a serious effort to use quantitative methods in political science. His book was published in 1928.[31] In 1930 came Harold Lasswell's *Psychopathology of Politics*.[32] In this book, he tried to use psychological categories for political studies. In a later work[33] he used the Freudian categories of the earlier work with his subsequent writings on power. William Munro saw physics as the proper model for a genuine political science. In an article, entitled "Physics and Politics : An Old Analogy Revised", he argued that the science and art of government still rests upon what may be called the atomic theory of politics – upon the postulate that all able bodied citizens were of equal weight, volume and value; enforced with inalienable rights; vested with the attribution of an indivisible sovereignty.[34]

The mood of these political scientists could be clearly understood from what Catlin wrote some three decades later. While restating his position Catlin said,

> The best guide (for the politicist as touching this relation of politics and Psychology) is perhaps to be found in the out look of that great and too little honoured man Graham Wallas, and in the pregnant remark of lord Bryce...in his *Modern Democracies 1921* : 'Politics has its roots in

30. G.E.C. Catlin *Science and Methods in Politics*, (New York, 1927).
31. Stuart, A. Rice, *Quantitative Methods in Politics*, (New York, 1928).
32. Harold Lasswell, *Psychopathology of Politics*, (New York, 1960. Originally published in 1930).
33. Harold Lasswell, *Power and Personality*, (New York, 1948).
34. W.B. Munro, "Physics and Politics : An Old Analogy Revised" *American Political Science Review*, Vol. XXII No. 1 (Feb., 1928), pp. 1-11.

Psychology', certainly this was the understanding which H.D. Lasswell and myself had years ago.[35]

Thus, under the leadership of Charles E. Merriam a formidable group of American Political Scientists attempted to build a science of politics with the help of Psychology and quantitative methods. It is evident from the writings of Merriam that the purpose of this approach was to muster the forces of political and social control. Their works have been fruitful as studies of political behaviour and political motivations as well as of the actual working of political institutions. But these political scientists accepted the fact-value dichotomy and argued that it was not a proper function of political scientists to teach how to be good democratic citizens.[36] They aimed at building up a value-free science of politics.

This position did not go unchallenged. William Y. Elliott, Edward S. Corwin and Charles, A. Beard pleaded against the possibilities as well as desirability of a value free science of politics. Elliott's *The Pragmatic Revolt in politics*[37] became very influential among some political scientists. It had been considered an appropriate counter to Catlin's *Science and Methods in Politics*. He was of the opinion that the general pre-occupation of political science in U.S.A. with descriptive studies of institutions and with attempts to formulate and apply an objective and purely scientific method to political studies might be intimately related to the fact that there was not a single contemporary political theorist in America who was to be counted among those of the first order. Elliott's own study aimed at supplying an approach to what he considered the central problem of contemporary political theory. He held that the problem centred around the issue of fact-value dichotomy. He undertook his study with the conviction that separation of facts and values could not bring any fruitful

35. G.E.G. Catlin, *Systematic Politics*, (Canada, 1962), p. 42.
36. This position has been made clear by Catlin. See G.E.G. Catlin, *Science and Methods in Politics, op. cit.*
37. W.Y. Elliott, *Pragmatic Revolt in Politics, op. cit.*

results.[38] He proposed to set all the problems of politics in their historical, economic and cultural environments instead of trying to work out a science of politics based on abstractions. He insisted that facts are shaped and used as they are interpreted and, therefore, students of politics must not ignore the problem of political values.[39] This book was a sharp critique of the current mood of the value-free political scientists. Elliott pointed out the weakness of that approach. He wrote :

> The Scientific method, to become a fruitful critique of moral values, must approach consequences themselves with this spider web of coherent logic and normative values. Otherwise it remains merely positivistic, behaviouristic, descriptive and morally blind.[40]

But Elliott himself did not make an attempt to theorize in the normative sense of the term. In his own words his aim was, "simply to run a thread of unity through the chief modern theories and experiments which are in revolt against political rationalism."[41] We have already pointed out that in the reformist phase of American political science, some political scientists wanted the discipline only to offer citizenship training; during the pragmatic era the followers of this school also opposed a value-free political science. Thomas H. Reed, for instance tried to draw the discipline closer to the earlier purposes of citizenship education. He was of the opinion that political science should train students for political and governmental careers. He was a protagonist of civil education and activism. This view was clearly stated in a book published jointly with Doris D. Reed. The authors wrote, "The object of this study is to suggest subject matter and methods which can be employed profitably in promoting

38. *Ibid.*, p. 5.

39. *Ibid.*, p. 51.

40. *Ibid.*, pp. 52-53.

41. *Ibid.*, p. vii.

better training for participation in politics."[42] Such suggestions were normative in nature. That is why Reed and his followers were also opposed to the concept of a value-free political science.

In this controversy over the desirability of a value-free science of politics on conclusive results were achieved. To quote Somit and Tananhaus, "Though neither Merriam nor Reed captured the holy land, or came close to it both crusades left their mark on the discipline".[43] These two groups of American Political Scientists opposed each other; but they had something in common too. Both of these groups either neglected the study of political theory or their approach to political science consequently resulted in a decline of political theory. One group was obsessed with methods and the other with citizenship training.

While this debate was going on and political theory was by and large neglected, a group of American political scientists took to the study of the ideas of the great political thinkers of the past. This trend was set by W.A. Dunning. He published his three volumes study entitled *A History of Political Theories* in 1902, 1905 and 1920 respectively. In these volumes Dunning wanted, "to present the interpretation of the development of political theory in its relation to political fact".[44] Easton rightly points out that in Dunning's hand the study of political theory is virtually converted into the history of political ideas and theories.[45] Dunning gave us a historical account of the conditions and consequences of political ideas. Another author MacIlwain considered politi-

42. Thomas H. Reed and Doris D. Reed, *Preparing College Men and Women for Politics*. (New York, 1952), p. 10. This study included a suggested syllabus for American citizenship.
43. A. Somit and J. Tananhaus : *The Development of American Political Science, From Burgess to Behaviouralism* (Boston 1967), p. 88.
44. W.A. Dunning : *A History of Political Theories : Ancient and Mediaeval* (New York, 1902), p. XXXV.
45. David Easton, Political System, *op. cit.*, p. 240.

eal ideas as effects of social activity. His *Growth of Political Thought in the West : From Greeks to the Middle Ages*[46] was also a general history of thought. Maclïwain's approach was different from that of Dunning in the sense that it emphasised an exploration of the historical conditions surrounding the emergence of an idea.[47] Unlike Dunning Mcllwain attributed special significance to moral judgements; but he was led to history as the most meaningful mode of interpreting moral ideas. To quote Easton, "In spite of his undoubted conviction that it is worthwhile to affirm moral views, his conception of the role of ideas in general bars him from advocating anything other than a historical treatment."[48]

A third author who adopted a similar approach was George H. Sabine. In the words of Easton Sabine agrees with Dunning that "the examination of political thought merits attention because it is an aspect of the political process that interacts with and influences social action. With the latter (Macllwain) he maintains the necessity of describing and analysing the moral judgements in each theory".[49] For Sabine every political theory could be examined from two points of view : as Social Philosophy and as ideology. Sabine accepted Humes Position on facts and values. Like Hume he holds, that no fact implies any other fact and no fact implies any value [50] Easton says :

> In such a study we ought to isolate the influence of a theory on the actions of men; this is the psychological aspect. We can analyze the factual statements implicit in any theory and set them against the facts as we know them

46, C.H. Mcllwain : *The Growth of Political Thought in the West : From Greeks to the Middle Ages* (New York, 1932).

47. David Easton, *The Political System, op. cit.*, p. 244.

48. *Ibid.*, p. 248.

49. *Ibid.*, p. 249.

50. J.R. Weinburg. "On Sabine's philosophy of value", in Milton R. Konowitz and Arthur E. Murphy (eds) *Essays in Political Theory* (New York & London 1948), p. 246.

today. In this respect political theory is concerned with empirical truth.[51]

In Sabines approach moral inquiry helped only in historical understanding. Sabine did not encourage the students of political theory to examine value-theory with a view to help him formulate his own moral out look.

As all these writers were textbook writers, their role as such should be distinguished from that of political theorists. None of them tried to build any political theory themselves. Arnold Brecht makes this point when he says that, these writers had a tendency to look to the great writings as the main reposition of theoretic effort. He maintains that in their hands the study of theory was mainly directed to criticism and evaluation of the contributions of other people. There was little effort to make the study of theory an exercise in theory construction.[52] Easton, however, overlooks this distinction and goes on to explain that the approach adopted by these authors contributed to the decline of political theory. He calls it, "Decline into historicism".[53] About these three authors he says that he has inquired into their approach because they are representative of research in this field. He goes on to say, "Political theorists are primarily *historicist* in their orientation. They do not use the history of values as a device to stipulate thought on a possible constructive redefinition of political goals"[54] (emphasis added). It is clear that Easton calls them 'historicist' because their approach to values does not help one to constructively redefine political goals. The point about their treatment of values may be valid but does that make these authors 'historicists'? Like all other terms, historicism also has come to acquire a specific meaning through usage. Nobody has done more in giving to the

51. Easton, *Political System*, op. cit., p. 251.

52. Arnold Brecht, *Political Theory: Foundations of Twentieth Century Political Thought*, (Bombay, 1965), p. 503.

53. Easton, *The Political System*, *op. cit.*, p. 234.

54. *Ibid.*, p. 253.

concept of historicism its accepted meaning than Karl Popper, according to whom:

> historicism (is) an approach to the social sciences which assumes that historical prediction is their principal aim, and which assumes that this aim is attainable by discovering the rhythms or the patterns, the laws or the trends that underline the evolution of history.[55]

None of the three eminent scholars mentioned above has anything to do with predicting the future. Probably what Easton meant was that they were applying a crude historical method. Easton himself shows that in their study of moral problems these authors turned to history largely for the sake of narration.[56] In this sense their approach cannot be designated as 'historicist.'

One may not agree with Easton when he calls these authors historicist, but he surely makes a point when he says that their approach was partly responsible for a decline in the study of political theory. They studied ideas of past, examined their antecedents and tried to understand them by placing them in their own historical situations; but never treated political theory in a manner which can increase our understanding of the world—present and future. In fact implicit in this approach was a withdrawal from the present. In the inter-war period American political scientists were confronted with a tense socio-political situation. They responded to it in two ways: while some of them tried to use a 'Scientific method' to acquire mastery over the social forces so that those could be controlled and the society could be saved from a crisis, others withdrew to the study of ideas of the great thinkers. Both of these trends neglected the study of political theory. The first emphasized technical skill, the other withdrew to the past.

55. Karl R. Popper, *The Poverty of Historicism* (London, 1957), p. 3.
56. Easton, *op. cit.*, p. 254.

The rise of Behaviouralism : A positivist view of political science

In the post war America also there was no remarkable improvement in the state of political theory. The victory in the war was accompanied by a series of problems both economic and political. The black market had flourished during the war and its activity increased with peace. The price level established by law remained relatively stable, but the actual costs paid by consumers soared. The businessmen could pass the increases on to the helpless consumers ; but the labourers felt the pinch of higher cost of living. Yet their demands for higher wages met the determined resistance of the employers. Faulkner shows that there was a desire to adopt a tough policy towards labour. A fear of dissenters and radicals prevailed in the atmosphere and there was a general swing towards the right.[57] If the American Social Seientists of this period had tried to critically examine the situation they would have found it necessary to raise normative questions regarding the system. Instead of doing this they decided to eschew normative questions and took refuge in what was called a "value-free social science". The philosophical basis of this brand of social inquiry already existed in logical positivism.

It was in this period that pragmatic philosophy suffered a set back and logical positivism started gaining ground. Logical positivism with its emphasis on the fact-value dichotomy suited those American social scientists of this period who had a status-quo bias and wanted to avoid fundamental questions of a normative nature. Logical positivists insisted on strictly "physicalist" or behaviouralist methods. They wanted elemination of metaphysical terms in all phases of research. They wanted to designate any statement which was not variable through perception as not only "non-scientific" but also meaningless.[58] This does not mean, however, that

57. See, H.U. Faulkner, *American Political and Social History* (New York, 1952), pp. 42-50.

58. See, Brecht, *op. cit.*, pp. 174-75.

they entirely neglected values. But these they were concerned with as individuals. As social scientists they felt that they were only concerned with facts.

All these ideas were founded upon the methodological position of fact-value dichotomy. According to this position statements about facts should be separated from statements about values and the subjective preferences of the observer. Associated with this is the idea of value-relativism—the idea that values are derived from life experiences of individuals and that superiority or inferiority of values cannot be decided on the basis of factual evidence.[59] These ideas were central to the rise of behaviouralism also. Easton, a leading exponent of Behaviouralism, argued that it shifted the balance of concern from prescription, ethical enquiry, and action to description, explanation and verification. He explained that "Behaviouralism has justified this shift on the grounds that without the accumulation of reliable knowledge, the means for the achievement of goals would be so uncertain as to convert action into a futile game."[60]

The pioneers of Behaviouralism in political science were highly critical of traditional political science which followed a historical, legal or normative approach. They pleaded that to acquire reliable knowledge political science must develop more fruitful modes of analysis. These arguments started as early as 1908. Graham Wallas and A.F. Bently were pioneers in this field. Wallas emphasized the importance of psychology and Bently drew the attention of the discipline to the process mode of analysis.[61] In 1913 Beard argued in his book "*An Economic Interpretation of the Constitution of the United States*[62] that the constitution grew out of the definite group

59. See, *Ibid.*, pp. 117-118.

60. Easton, *The Political System, op. cit.*, p. 328.

61. Wallas, *Human Nature in Politics, op. cit.* Bently, *The Process of Government, op. cit.*

62. Charles A. Beard, *An Economic Interpretation of the Constitution of the United States* (New York, 1913).

conflicts. These path-breaking studies were by and large ignored by the contemporary political scientists because the discipline at that time as we have already noted, was engrossed in matters of practical importance. Arguments on these lines were carried on by authors like Charles E. Merrian, Harold Gosnel, Harold Lasswell. In 1950's these books began to gain currency and Behaviouralism established itself firmly in political science. As Vandyke has pointed out, "A behavioural approach is distinguishd predominately by the nature of the purpose it is designed to serve. The purpose is scientific."[63] The behaviouralists view of science is of course value-free. Heinz Eulau says, "It is the function of science to understand and interpret the world not to change it."[64] The implication is clear. If the scientist endeavours to change the world he will have to make value judgements; if he merely interprets he can afford to remain value-free. Eaulau, further, states that the great issues of politics such as the conditions and consequences of freedom, justice or authority are admittedly significant topics ; but they are topics compounded with a strong dose of metaphysical discourse. He does not think that they are beyond the reach of behavioural investigation; but before they can be tackled the ground work must be laid.[65] This task of laying the ground work oriented the discipline to factual research. As a result the normative questions became almost out of bound for behavioural political science. The urge to build a science of politics seized the minds of the American political scientists in such a manner that they sought to emulate the natural sciences in building what was conceived to be a field of knowledge anchored in facts. Such an approach cannot be fruitful in social sciences including political science, because it ignores the qualitative uniqueness of the social form of movements and developments. In fact it glosses over the differences between human society and the

63. Vernon Vandyke, *Political Science : A Philosophical Analysis* (Standford California, 1960), p. 159.

64. Heinz Eulau, *Behavioural Persuasion in Politics* (Bombay 1963), p. 10.

65 *Ibid*, pp. 10-11.

world of nature. Moreover, if one attempts to develop a field of knowledge anchored in facts one is necessarily confined to those aspects of social and political events that lend themselves to precise description, repeated observation, quantification, and other such objective treatment. This leads to trivilization of political science. A Political Science that depends solely on facts and factual knowledge could afford to neglect political theory. This view of political science which Easton later called "Hyperfactualism"[66] siphoned away energy from seeing the facts in their theoretical significance.[67] As a result the development of political science was seriously affected. Vandyke rightly says that this purpose of scientific work is surely among the obstacles to the development of a science of politics. The strong tendency has been simply to gather facts and to write and teach for the sake of facts. In this way, under the influence of behaviouralism post war American Political Science fell into the abyss of hyperfacturalism.

The behaviouralists were not completely blind to the dangerous aspects of this trend. Some of them did take pains to explain that they did not ignore the question of values. Eulau for instance argued that he did not claim that science could not investigate preferences, values, or policy objectives because it could not tell us what good was best or what action was just. He did not believe that those things were any more inscrutable than more mundane matters of political behaviour.[68] It would appear that these scientists do take values into consideration ; but their actual position becomes clear when we notice that in practice they try to leave the questions of value alone. Eulau argues that the goal is man ; but like a true behaviouralist he refuses to say what kind of man. He writes, "these are philosophical questions better left to the philosophers. Whatever answer one chooses, there is likely to be a corresponding predicament."[69]

66. Easton, *op. cit.*, p. 66.
67. See, *Ibid.*, pp. 77-78.
68. Eulau, *op. cit.*, pp. 145-146.
69. *Ibid.*, p. 144.

This reluctance of the behavioural scientists to deal with such questions emanates from their belief that it is not possible to make final judgements about human values, Eulau for instance says,

> The question of *whether a value-free science of politics is possible must not be confused with the question of whether a value-free science is desirable.* The former is a problem of fact that in the end can be answered only through empirical research into the nature of science as a form of human activity. *The later is a problem of value that will remain open as long as scientists themselves give different answers.* I think it will remain an open question for generations to come"[70] (emphasis added).

Here he is arguing that since the possibility or impossibility of a value-free science is a question of fact its truth could be empirically verified ; but desirability is a question of value and therefore could not be empirically verified. Eulau and others like him are interested in building a 'Science of Politics' based on empirical investigation. The positivist view of social sciences led behavioural political scientists to a study of facts for the sake of facts themselves, and as a result political theory remained neglected during the post war American political science also.

Our discussion above shows that since its inception in the post civil war period American Political Science has travelled through the stages of reformism, pragmatism, scientism and Behaviouralism. In all these stages of development American Political Science neglected the study of political theory. The discipline was engrossed in practical problems of training citizens, suggesting reforms or collecting facts to build a science anchored in facts. Critical Political thinking in America prior to the emergence of American political science came from men like Madison, Hamilton, Paine and Jefferson.[71]

70. *Ibid.*, pp. 146-147.

71. See, Vernon Louis Parrington, *Main Currents in American Thought*, (New York, 1958), Vol. I, Book III, Parts I & II.

Even after the emergence of political science critical thinking regarding political matters have been there.[72] But such thinking did not lead to formulation of any theory and the discipline of political science had failed to develop any political theory worth the name. It is, therefore, difficult to accept Easton's contention that there was decline of Political theory in America. In fact, the study of political theory in American Political Science never really took off. The roots of the neglect of political theory in American political science, as we have tried to show, could be found in the socio-political atmosphere in which the discipline emerged and developed. One may not agree with Easton on this point, but one must appreciate the fact that he was one of the few political scientists who emphasized the need for a serious study of political theory. Easton hoped to win back for theory its proper and necessary place. In the next chapter we examine Easton's treatment of political theory to assess his contribution in this direction.

72. *Ibid.,* Vol. III.

[illegible] after the emergence of political science critical think-[illegible] political enquiry had been there.[illegible] But it was [illegible] to formulation of any theory and the [illegible] political science had failed to develop any point of theory worth the name. It is, therefore, difficult to accept [illegible] contention that there was decline of Political theory [illegible] the study of political theory in American Political Science never really took off. The roots of the [illegible] of political theory in American political science, as we have tried to show, could be found in the socio-political atmosphere in which the discipline emerged and developed. We may not agree with Easton on this point, but one must appreciate the fact that he was one of the [illegible] political scientists who emphasized the need for a serious study of political theory. [illegible] back for theory its [illegible] place. In the next chapter, we examine Easton's treatment of political theory to assess his contribution in this direction.

Ibid., Vol. III.

CHAPTER 3

Heterogeneity of Facts and Values : Empirical Theory of David Easton

We have shown in the preceding chapter that the problems arising out of the neglect of political theory is one of the central themes of Easton's political science. He has drawn the attention of the practitioners of the discipline to what he calls the "historicist" and the "hyperfuctuatist" tendencies of American political science. He holds, that these trends led to the decline of political theory in America. He, however, points out that there have been some attempts at formulating a body of political theory to guide research. Such attempts led political scientists to the formulation of a framework that he calls "the theory of political equilibrium".[1] Easton explains that in political science the idea of equilibrium is used in two different senses. (1) General equilibrium, and (2) Constitutional equilibrium. The general equilibrium, in turn, conveys two ideas. First, that all elements or variables in a political system are functionally inter-dependent; and second, that they will tend to act and react on each other to

1. Easton, *The Political System*, *op. cit.*, p. 267.

a point where a state of stability, if even for a moment obtains.[2]

The concept of inter-dependence is closely related to the idea of a political process. As we have seen in the preceding chapter this idea was introduced to American Political Science by A.F. Bently.[3] Once the notion of process with its pluralist causal assumptions crept into the political research it was easy for the idea of equilibrium already familiar in economics and sociology to filter in as well. The idea of equilibrium implies that there is a tendency to maintain the given equilibrium. Easton shows that the argument of Bently's *Process of Government* implies that the process tends to maintain itself in a system and that the law and the governmental institutions or the formal expression of policy and the high level agencies framing this policy, were all intertwined with underlying groups in a complex reaction system that constantly tended towards a moment of balance or equilibrium.[4]

The influence of the equilibrium concept on the American Political Scientists has been rather, obvious. As Easton says, "a reading of significant empirical literature in the United States since the first world war reveals the astonishing extent to which the equilibrium notion has been adopted."[5] Easton further shows how this concept has been used some times to refer to an actual condition that occurs at some moment in time; and how at other times it has been used to describe an equilibrating or balancing tendency.[6] The first meaning leaves the impression that activities which are functionally interrelated act and react until they ultimately reach a condition wherein no actor is willing to change his position in relation to theirs. Easton bases his analysis of this idea on Catlin's writings who uses the idea to mean a condition of rest. He

2. *Ibid.*, p. 268.
3. Bently, *op. cit.*
4. Easton, *op. cit.*, pp. 270-71.
5. *Ibid.*, p. 272.
6. *Ibid.*, p. 274.

believes that the essential homogeneity of political relations lies in the fact that each person in society, and each group, seeks to assert his or its will over others through control or power over them. But he argues that to live together is as fundamental as individual assertiveness. He writes, "in the political act ..., the primary object is to procure some personal adjustment of the will of another man to my will ..."[7] Catlin argues that the political process, thus, consists of the means and paths whereby these conflicting wills are brought into some sort of 'Consensus', 'harmony', 'balance', or 'equilibrium'. Catlin does not distinguish between these terms. But Easton points out that if any set of political relations are the product of adjustment of wills at the time, when these relations change the old equilibrium will be destroyed to make way for a new one.[8] In this sense Catlin seems to have contradicted himself. Moreover, Easton rightly says that to prove that an empirical system ever reaches a condition of rest and to discover that the change has stopped the term equilibrium will have to be defined sharply which Catlin could not do.

The term equilibrium has not always been used to mean a state of rest, Easton says, "Conventionally equilibria are classified as stationery or dynamic".[9] Charles E. Merriam used the concept in a dynamic sense. Merriam argues that the social situation constantly involves the maintenance of 'equilibrium' between groups, classes and factions. In Merriam's view politics, therefore, involves 'reconciling of interests' or it calls for a 'balance'.[10] This balance is, however, not viewed as a static one. He views political action as something which is living and on the move. He says, "It is possible to have a clearer understanding of the basic

7. G.E.G. Catlin, *A Study of the Principles of Politics*, (London, 1930), p. 71.
8. Easton, *op. cit.*, pp. 275-77.
9. David Easton, "Limits of the Equilibrium Model in Social Research" in H, Eulau, G.J.M. Eldervel, M. Janowitz (ed.) *Political Behaviour* (Illinois, 1956), p. 399.
10. C.E. Merriam, *Systematic Politics* (Chicago 1945), p. 8.

necessities which government satisfies by examining both the typical complexes which call for political action and the conditioning elements in which it *lives* and moves"[11] (emphasis added). Merriam does not explain the idea in details, but he repeatedly refers to what he calls "moving equilibrium"[12]. Easton rightly argues that in depicting the equilibrium as one that moves, Merriam must mean that at certain stages in the process moments of equilibrium do occur.[13] He therefore concludes that these political scientists in fact tried to convert a useful tool of analysis into a misleading picture of reality.[14] It is surprising that a perceptive scholar like Easton fails to realise that even if these scholars used equilibrium as a tool of analysis and tried consciously to prevent its conversion into what Easton calls, a misleading picture of reality; they would have failed miserably. Because tools of analysis we use for social analysis entail one or more hypotheses about the social reality. These hypotheses are in fact tentative suggestions about social reality. Whether he consciously does so or not, when a social scientist chooses a tool of analysis he makes a choice about an attendant notion of reality. Therefore it is not right to say that political scientists like Merriam converted equilibrium, a tool of analysis into a picture of reality rather they chose equilibrium as a tool because they had a particular notion of reality. We shall discuss this point at details in a later chapter.

However, Easton shows that when political scientists like Bently used this idea of equilibrating tendency they viewed the process as one steadily striving to achieve a moment of equilibrium which was never attained. This approach seems to enhance the utility of the concept because here the reality is not viewed as an equilibrium. Easton points out that even this approach would face the problem of quantification. Some

11. *Ibid.*, p. 1.
12. See, C.E. Merriam, *The Role of Politics in Social Change,* (New York 1936). In this book he uses the phrase repeatedly.
13. Easton, *op. cit.*, pp. 279-80.
14. *Ibid.*, p. 250.

of the most important variables relevant to the study of politics are not quantifiable at least not at the present state of the science. Power, for instance, is a variable which is difficult to measure. Easton makes the point succinctly when he says, "Lacking appropriate indices for the measurement of power much of the usefulness of the point of equilibrium as a theoretical norm disappears."[15] But even if this problem is overcome there is still another major problem—the problem of numbers. The relevant variables in the study of a political process are so numerous that such an analysis becomes almost impossible. To quote Easton "The multiplicity of variables, even if they could be satisfactorily quantified, would still place formidable barriers in the way of rewarding equilibrium analysis."[16]

Easton maintains that in spite of these limitations the equilibrium concept has some value at the level of insights. The description of a political process as an equilibrium suggests that this process takes place in a political system. The idea of a system implies that the parts of the process are mutually dependent and therefore any change in one part will influence the rest of the system. The resulting changes will, in turn, react back on the element stimulating the initial change. It insists on plural factor causation. Viewing political life as a system would also imply that the interrelated parts of this system tend to cohere. Such a coherant whole will be distinguishable from other related phenomena. At the level of insight then such a view of the political life enables the political scientist to distinguish and therefore identify political phenomena from among the whole mass of social phenomena. This identification helps the political scientist immensely to simplify the reality. Simplification of reality is, of course, a task of theory.

Easton is of the opinion that the idea of moving equilibrium does not rule out the possibilities of change. In fact

15. *Ibid.*, p. 288.
16. *Ibid.*, p. 290.

it views political life as a process that keeps on moving from one point of equilibrium to another. Easton, therefore, argues that such an approach maintains at the fore-front of political inquiry the problem of political change. He holds that it should serve to keep alive the importance of studying political change.[17] We shall turn to this point presently.

Easton, then, goes on to analyse the idea of the constitutional equilibrium. Here, he shows that it presented itself in many forms. In Mosca's *'The Ruling Class'* this concept was used to imply that an equilibrium among social classes would permit rule of law. Sometimes this concept is used to include a balance among social groups also. Yet another form is cited by Easton in the point made by the federalists that a social equilibrium is insufficient. The separation of power is, therefore, designed to introduce an equilibrium within the legal structure.[18] The form in which it is manifested in international politics emphasises that peace depends upon an appropriate balance of power. Easton explains that constitutional equilibrium assumes that equilibrium facilitates maintenance of order; but he points out that there is no concrete data to prove or disprove this.

From the above discussion it is clear that in his assessment of both the general and constitutional equilibrium, Easton maintains that, the idea of quantification is inalienable from the concept of equilibrium. He argues that as quantification of political data is not possible, at least at the present stage of the science this concept can't be used as a tool of analysis. He, however, sees its utility in keeping alive the importance of studying political change. Easton seems to have missed the main issue involved in the question of application of equilibrium analysis in political science or for that matter in all social sciences. Despite all the ideas of disequilibrium and moving equilibrium this concept always betrays a bias in favour of the maintenance of the status-quo. Even in econo-

17. *Ibid*, p. 292.

18. *Ibid.*, p. 294.

mics and sociology, from where Easton says the concept has crept into political science, it has a conservative effect.

In economics equilibrium theory was the result of a reaction to the classical economics. The neo-classical economics of this brand tried to explain that it was the utility of a particular commodity which determined its value.[19] "These theories focussed on the market relations with determination in exchange of relative prices took over as the primary and principal theme and thereby replaced the primacy of production relations".[20] In this brand of economic theory equilibrium is defined in terms of the relationship between supply and demand and occurs where the two intersect. A movement from the equilibrium position occurs through alterations in amounts demanded and supplied. Changes in any other variable such as time, the nature of conditions or tastes cause a movement to a new situation, and, therefore, a fresh position of equilibrium. This process can be repeated indefinitely but it all takes place within an unaltered system of freemarket economy.[21] A freemarket is a prerequisite of equilibrium analysis. The question of the transition of the system of freemarket distribution to another economic system is beyond the scope of this framework. To that extent it has a conservative effect.

In sociology too, this framework reflects a similar bias. Sociology seems to have borrowed the concept from physiology.[22] In sociology equilibrium means that everybody plays his role. Though some equilibrium theorists hold that consensus on values is a prime feature of the social system not

19. W.S. Jevons, *The Theory of Political Economy*, (New Jersey, 1911), p. 77.
20. Krishna Bharadwaj, *Classical Political Economy and Rise to Dominance of Supply and Demand Theories* (New Delhi, 1978), p. 35.
21. See, V.L. Allen, *Social Analysis : A Marxist Alternative* (London and New York, 1975), p. 174.
22. See, Cynthia Russett. *Concept of Equilibrium in American Social Thought* (New York, 1966).

all of them agree to this but in one way or another they all regard the exercise of power as an exchange in which all citizens participate and which makes it possible to think of society as a system held in equilibrium. There may be disturbances which may produce failure of communication with the system; but the system is regarded as persisting through time by virtue of the equilibrium created either by its internal cycles of power and support, or by the inter-change between sub-systems as mediated by the currency of power.[23] In this sense equilibrium does not mean stability. An equilibrium may be stable, unstable or neutral, depending upon the relationship between the elements which are defined as constituting equilibrium. But in all its forms this equilibrium position is seen as the stable and therefore the desired one.

Some political scientists have been able to note this conservative effect of equilibrium analysis. Spragen shows that the present tendency of equilibrium analysis is to imply a kind of conservation. He writes "throughout its history...one feature of the concept of equilibrium has remained quite consistent—namely its perception as an essentially desirable situation. Such diverse figures as Comte, Spencer, Ward, Parato, Bently and Catlin have agreed on this".[24] In equilibrium analysis one has to talk about the equilibrium of related variables such as supply and demand, goals, social control, or sentiments and interests, or whatever are regarded as the prime determinants of behaviour. It would make no sense of the concept to do otherwise. Allen argues that in this framework the very choice of the variables carries with it a stability bias. When they are in harmony then they are in equilibrium and there is stability. Disequilibrium is equated with disharmony and conflict. A consequence of the use of equilibrium analysis has been to emphasize that a change away from any given

23. See, Ralf Dahrendorf, *Essays in the Theory of Society* (London, 1968), pp. 113-128 and 137-150.

24. T.A. Spragen, *The Dilemma of Contemporary Political Theory Toward a Post-Behavioural Science of Politics* (New York, 1973), p. 84.

equilibrium position must have negative or derogatory effects. It is but one step away from claiming that change itself is undesirable. Thus, equilibrium analysis is *status quo* analysis.[25] Easton overlooks this bias and praises the concept for its utility at the level of insight. He, however expresses his dissatisfaction for its dependence on quantification.

Easton has correctly pointed out the failure of American political science to develop any political theory in the real sense of the term. He, does not say that absence of theory makes empirical generalisation impossible. He only emphasises that to attain a high degree of reliability of knowledge theory is a necessity.[26] Easton, therefore, pleads for a revival of political theory. But the question is what kind of a theory? Easton divides political theory into two broad categories (1) The value theory, (2) Causal theory. According to him value theory discusses political values or the philosophy of politics causal theory seeks to show the relations among political facts.[27] Easton emphasizes the importance of value theory. In an essay mentioned above he wrote that political theory by tradition had chosen as part of its task to try to propose standards within the framework of which practical policy might be adopted.[28] But as we have seen in the preceding chapter he held that towards the end of the nineteenth century, however, interest in the reformulation of values and in conception of a good political order declined. He went on to suggest "... new vision and clarity for research is possible if the political scientist is trained to appraise his values critically."[29] He thinks that this will ensure the relevance and significance of political research for human goals.

In '*The Political System*' also he asserted that a neglect of value theory had affected political science in an adverse

25. Allen, *op. cit.*, p. 102.
26. Easton, *The Political System*, op. cit., p. 66.
27. *Ibid.*, pp. 53-54 and 78-79.
28. Easton, 'decline of political theory', *op. cit.*, p. 43.
29. *Ibid*, p. 50.

manner. He argued that political scientists must take a constructive approach toward the question of values.[30] In his famous presidential address to the 65th annual meeting of the American political association he reviewed the achievements of behaviouralism in political science and held, "Today the hazards of neglecting our normative presuppositions are all too apparent."[31] He argued in favour of creative speculations. In the epelogue 'B' to the second edition of *The Political System,* he claims that he sought to reconstruct the image of science so as to justify the inclusion of creative moral discourse and dispute within the boundaries of the scientific enterprise itself.[32] But a close analysis of his writings shows that in the ultimate analysis his political theory is only Causal theory, which he calls empirical theory.

Easton's preference for empirical theory to value theory is reflected in his treatment of the relation between facts and values. He views the factual aspect of a proposition as one that refers to a part of the reality. Therefore, it can be tested by reference to the facts. In this way its truth could be checked. The moral aspect is viewed as one that expresses the emotional response of an individual to a state to which an individual desires a particular state of affairs to exist. He says, "Although we can say that the aspect of a proposition referring to a fact can be true or false it is meaningless to characterise, the value aspect of a proposition in this way".[33] Such an approach does not exclude value questions from the scope of scientific research right away. They can be examined as observable facts associated with human activity. What it forbids is value judgements. The scientist may take account of values but he cannot decide whether a particular set of values is preferable to others.

An examination of Easton's ideas about the causal or

30. Easton, *The Political System, op. cit.*, pp. 220-232.
31. *Ibid.*, p. 338.
32. *Ibid.*, p. 360.
33. *Ibid.*, p' 221.

empirical theory will throw more light on his views on the questions of values and value theories. Easton is aware of the fact that there is no such thing as a pure fact. The interest of the observer always determines the selection of facts about any event. Such a selection is made on the light of a frame or reference that fixes the order and relevance of the facts. "When raised to the level of consciousness this frame of reference is what we call a theory".[34] Such a theory would, of course, be a causal theory. Easton divides causal theory into three types. This division is based on the scope of such theories. These types are :

1. **Singular generalizations :**

These are statements of observed uniformities between two isolated and easily identified variables. From these, few deductions can be made that go beyond the actual observed uniformity. These are not theories in the strict sense.

2. **Synthetic narrow gauge theory :**

These are at a higher intermediary level. They consist of sets of inter-related propositions that are designed to synthesise the data contained in an unorganized body of singular generalizations. But in this process the theory that is developed goes beyond the actual data included in the original cluster of generalizations.

3. **Broad gauge or systematic theory :**

This is the conceptual framework within which a whole discipline is cast.[35]

This conceptual framework is considered by Easton as the empirical theory that a discipline must develop to produce reliable knowledge. Easton describes it as a sieve which helps to sort out, select and reject observed facts ; or a compass

34. *Ibid.*, p. 53.
35. *Ibid.*, p. 53-57.

which indicates the direction in which research is moving ; or a gauge which reports the state of development of a science at a particular time. Such a framework is flexible in nature. He writes, "it is a body of theory which changes in the light of the facts that it collects or that suggest it".[36] Easton explains that each investigator while undertaking an analysis within a given field, uses some theories and assumptions. The conceptual framework consists of these theories and assumptions. A conceptual framework helps the researcher to test the relevance of succeeding research. There is nothing sacrosanct about such a framework. Its utility in understanding phenomena is its supreme test. Greater the variety of significant problems that it can help to unify and give meaning to, better is the framework. Such is the idea that Easton propagates about a mature theory of political science. It is a theory which is based on a few basic, empirically derived premises. It is a theory which facilitates the formulation of intermediate theories based on deductions. His idea of this kind of an empirical theory and its role is based on his understanding of the role of theory in physics and economics.[37] He hopes, "it is conceivable that some day in the social sciences such a framework might reach the stage of maturity associated with theory in physics, for example".[38] Easton argues that such a framework makes it possible for a discipline to formulate deductively a whole body of intermediate theory. This makes the prediction of empirical events possible. Prediction of empirical events is very important for political science of Eastonian brand ; because his concept of political science is similar to the prediction-generalization model of science. Easton wants to build a general science of politics. He also wants to predict how a political system will behave in a particular situation. As Thorson puts it, "One cannot even follow his arguments, make sense of his transitions, let alone accept his conclusions, unless one at least understands the prediction-generalization concep-

36. *Ibid.*, p. 57.

37. See *Ibid.*, pp. 57-58.

38. *Ibid* , p. 58.

tion of science."[39] His idea of political theory as a conceptual framework suits the purpose of such a science.

Easton spells out three reasons for which such a framework is essential for an adequate analysis of the Political system ; (1) Through such a theory it would be possible to identify the significant political variables and describe their mutual relations, (2) It facilitates comparison of research and maps out areas in which additional or new research is badly needed, (3) It adds to the reliability of the results of both new and old research.[40] Easton, therefore, considers such a framework to be the highest form of empirical theory necessary for political science. The emphasis thus laid on such a theory leads him to a situation where he concentrates on the possibilities of developing such a framework and devotes most of his work since 1965 towards this end. As a result normative political theory is relegated to the background. Even the explanatory tasks of political theory are forgotten. As Meehan says, "Easton does not think of a political theory in terms of explanations but in terms of the creation of conceptual framework."[41]

As we have noted above, Easton does not only not ignore but emphasises the importance of value theory but in his own political science we do not see such a theory. His is an empirical political science. His political theory is also empirical political theory only. In the face of his own neglect of value theory and the role that he gives to empirical theory, his deliberations on the need of value theory becomes a mere lip service. This becomes evident from what he has to say about the state of political theory in Pre-world War II period. "The dominance of historical and ethical theory had at that time virtually crushed out any small shoots of empirical theory that

39. Thomas Landon Thorson, *Bio·politics, op. cit.,* p. 58.

40. Easton, *Political System*, op. cit., pp. 61-62.

41. Eugene Meehan, *Contemporary Political Thought : A Critical Study*, op. cit., p. 173.

had reached the surface prior to world war II".[42] In another place he says :

> Prior to world war II, theory almost exclusively implied moral philosophy in its various forms or, at the very least the history and analysis of the moral systems of the great political thinkers of the past. *Only the barest glimmerings of the modern kind of theory were visible.* For most students of politics, the little that did exist was scarcely recognizable as such, very seldom was it clearly identified and labelled"[43] (emphasis added).

This modern kind of theory here refers to empirical theory. Easton notices that after the world war II political theory has undergone a major revolution. He maintains that the image of political theory built in the philosophical tradition of Plato, Aristotle, Rousseau, Mill or Dewey is giving way. "The aspect ...which now rises to shatter the old image of the nature and tasks may be described as a descriptive, empirically oriented, behavioural, operational or causal".[44]

Easton, thus, emphasises the role of empirical theory. This itself is not objectionable. In fact it is necessary to recognise the importance of such a theory. Easton's arguments for taking such theory seriously must be considered as a contribution to the development of political science. But he not only emphasizes the need for such theories but also views them separately from normative theory and goes on to build such a theory for political science in the form of systems analysis. If we accept Easton's conceptual framework we will be building a set of political theories which will be empirical in nature. And if we follow his arguments for the need of value theory then may

42. David Easton, *A Framework of Political Analysis*, (New Jersey, 1965), p. ix.

43. David Easton "Alternative Strategies in theoretical research", in David Easton (ed), *Varieties of Political Theory* (New Jersey, 1967) p. 1.

44. David Easton, *A System Analysis of Political Life*. (New York, 1965), p. 5.

be, we will be building another set of theories which are normative in nature. This idea of separating value and empirical theories ring bells of positivism in one's mind. Influence of positivism on Easton has already been pointed out. Dante Germino, for instance, brands him as an axiological positivist. Axiological positivists are those, who while agreeing that value judgements are not and may not become scientific, nevertheless insist upon the propriety and indeed inalienability of value speculations on the part of the social scientist. Because it is not possible to achieve a completely value-free social science. It is maintained that the investigator should frankly state and develop his value assumptions, carefully labelling them as such.[45]

In fairness to Easton it must be noted here that he does not consider a mere formal statement of the value premises of the researcher as sufficient. He says, "...it is deceptive however, to accept formal assertion of belief in certain moral postulates as a meaningful description of the ethical premises behind theoretical research".[46] Easton is aware of the fact that such a formal statement cannot give an accurate picture of the moral views of the theorist. He, therefore, suggests that theorists should take a constructive approach toward moral clarification. This approach requires more than a mere formal statement of the values of the theorist. Easton says that, "A constructive approach requires the synthesis of values with facts to bring out the full meaning of the values".[47]

Faston argues that this approach has always been followed by all the great philosophers of the past. He says that an analysis of the components of any political theory shows how a theorist communicates his values, not through the assertion of a few dogmatic premises, but through the elaborate construction of the consequences of his moral views for the politi-

45. Germino, *Beyond Ideologv, op. cit.*, p. 69.
46. Easton, *The Political System, op. cit.*, p. 232.
47. *Ibid.*, p. 231.

cal structure and processes.[48] If a constructive approach can synthesize values and facts and can show the consequences of the moral views of the theorist, it probably is the best we can do to solve the problem of the fact-value dichotomy. But unfortunately this does not happen. Easton has not been able to come out of the clutches of positivism. There is no doubt that he emphasized the importance of values and value theory; but he wants the theorist to save his theory from the impact of his own moral views. Easton writes, "...the theorist cannot check the impact of his moral views on his theory unless he is thoroughly aware of these views".[49] The implications of this positions are unmistakable. If Easton wants the theorist to save his (theorists) theories from being influenced by his moral views, he is assuming that it is possible and desirable to separate values from facts.

The separation of fact and value is the basic methodological postulate of positivism. Easton's adherence to this position becomes clear from what he says in 1971 in his epilogue 'B' to the second edition of the *Political System*: "I sought to construct the image of science so as to justify the inclusion of creative moral discourse and dispute within the boundaries of the scientific enterprise itself and not only within the university, *while continuing to accept the logical heterogeneity of facts and values*".[50] (emphasis added).

Easton, then, continues to adhere to the logical heterogeneity of facts and values. This methodological position has led social scientists to what is generally known as value-neutrality. In modern social sciences this idea is associated with the name of Max Weber.[51] Irving Horrowitz shows how the weberian idea has been further developed by his followers and how the course of events identified social science not only with value

48. *loc. cit.*
49. *Ibid.*, p. 232,
50. *Ibid.*, p. 350.
51. For a discussion on this point See, Frohock, *op. cit.*, p. 146.

neutrality but with scholarly aloofness from moral issues.[52] This position about values is based on the belief that natural science is the model or pattern for social sciences. The natural sciences could apparently be independent of values prevailing in society. Social scientists who hope to build such social sciences believe that this independence is attainable in social sciences also. We have already noted that Easton's idea of political theory is based on his understanding of the role of theory in physics. Therefore, he also falls into this trap. His political science, like the social sciences of those who adhere to this view, does not permit the political scientist to make value judgements. A methodology based on counter posing judgements of facts to value judgements implies that political science is not capable of choosing value alternatives. It believes that science can only say how to achieve goals ; but cannot say which goal is preferable. This approach regards political science as a neutral discipline and does not allow political scientists to draw any political, ideological or moral conclusions. It attempts at standing above politics and as a result confines itself to the study of what Christian Bay calls "pseudo-politics".[53] Bay rightly says, "we cannot avoid the realm of normative issues unless we really wish to disclaim all political significance for our work."[54]

If Easton is advocating the construction of a set of theories which are free from the influence of the moral views of the theorist he seems to believe that it is possible to deal with facts without getting involved in normative issues. He seems to be unaware of the fact that facts cannot even be described without a perspective. When a reseacher chooses a particular problem for study he makes a value choice. Such a choice cannot be made without some political or moral considera-

52. Irving Horrowitz (ed.) *The New Sociology : Essays in Social Science and Social Theory in Honour of C. Wright & Mills* (New York, 1964), p. 9.

53. Christian Bay. "Politics and Pseudo Politics : A Critical evaluation of some behavioural literature", in Mccoy and J. Playford (eds.) *A Political Politics.* (New York, 1967), p. 16.

54. *Loc. cit.*

tions. Moreover, all political knowledge is made for application. Even if the researcher manages to formulate his conclusions in a manner which appears to be value neutral, these become value-laden in the hands of those who make use of such knowledge. That is why it is not possible to develop an empirical political theory which is free from value biases at least not about really vital social problems.

Social theories are always influenced by the value preferences of the theorists Mydral has shown that the value connotation of our main concepts represents our interest in a matter, gives direction to our thoughts and significance to our inferences. He rightly concludes that there is no way of studying social reality other than from the view point of human ideals.[55] In this sense Easton's hope of developing a set of theories which are empirical in nature and on which the influence of the moral views of the theorist can be checked will remain a mere hope. An approach which requires the political theorist to state his moral position clearly to enable him check the influence of his moral views on his theory would develop only such theories which will be concerned only with description of the trivialities. It would prevent the theorist from studying the really vital social problems. And a political science built with the help of such theories will not be able to deal with questions like whether a particular social order is just or unjust ? or whether a change is or is not necessary ? Since the days of Greek Philosophers, the right order of society has traditionally been a central question of political theory. Easton's approach places it outside the scope of political theory. Theory thus becomes a hand maiden of empirical research. An analysis of Eastons major works will show that as a result of this conception of Political theory his political science becomes descriptive in nature. Such a science, of course, makes it possible for the scientist to ignore questions of normative nature.

55. Gurnar Myrdal in Paul Streeten (ed.) *Values in Social Theory : A Selection of Essays on Methodology*, (London, 1958), pp. 1-54.

CHAPTER 4

Definition of Politics: The Jevonian Revolution in Political Science

Our analysis of Easton's concept of political theory has shown that despite his protestations he remains firmly in lines with logical positivism so far as the question of fact-value dichotomy is concerned. His definition of politics re-inforces this position. Any attempt to build a political theory assumes that it is possible to define what is political. David Easton while arguing for a revival of political theory, therefore, had to define political phenomena and distinguish it from other social phenomena. He observes that political scientists feel quite instinctively that research into the political aspect of life does sufficiently differ from inquiry into any other aspects of social life to constitute a separate intellectual enterprise. He points out that political scientists have been acting on the unexpressed premise that the phenomena of politics tend to cohere. He says, "Such phenomena, form, in other words, a system which is part of the total social system and, yet which for purposes of analysis and research, is temporarily set apart".[1] He argues that it is artificial to isolate a set of social relations from the whole; but it is necessary for a simplification of political data. He further argues that politi-

1. Easton, *Political System*, *op. cit.*, pp. 96-97.

cal life could be looked upon as a sub-system which can be profitably examined, temporarily, apart from the whole social system.[2] But viewing political life as a system does not solve the problem. Politics has to be defined.

The absence of an universally accepted definition of politics has been a perrenial problem of political science. Since the days of the ancient Greek philosophers, scholars interested in the study of politics have been trying to define politics. As Herman Heller puts it, "the manifold constructs of political science and the controversy over its true content and method are not essentially different today from what they were in Hellenistic antiquity".[3] Heller rightly points out that in Greek antiquity study of politics revealed, in content as well as in method, a marked diversity and range. Speculations in the field of political studies were in the nature of a guide to political power, a course of civic training, a moral philosophy, a historical metaphysics, a sociology or some other type of special discipline. These aspects of political science are to be found even today.[4] As Easton shows, despite this diversity by the mid-twentieth century two widely different sets of criteria have emerged for differentiating political life from all other aspects of society and, thereby for isolating the subject matter of political science. These are—

(1) Institutional criteria; which attempts to define politics in terms of either the governmental institutions or the state;

(2) Functional criteria which attempts to define politics in terms of power or decision making.[5]

2. *Ibid.*, p. 97.
3. Herman Heller, "Political Science", in Edwin R.A. Seligman (ed.) *The EncyclopeDia of the Social Sciences* (New York, 1933), Vol. XI, p. 207.
4. *Ibid.*, p. 208.
5. David Eason, Political Science", in David L. Sills. (ed.) *International Encyclopedia of Social Sciences*, (New York, 1968), Vol. 12, p. 283.

Political science has very often been described as the study of governmental or political institutions.[6] Political scientists following this approach may find it easy to identify the institutions with which they are concerned but it is rather difficult to define the governmental institutions. Vandyke asks "What are the attributes of a government or of an agency or a sub-division of a government that justify the use of the label?"[7] Unless the terms governmental and political can be defined this approach cannot throw any light on the problem of differentiating political life from all other aspects of social life. To quote Easton "We are left as much in the dark about the subject matter of political life as ever, that is at the mercy of our institutions."[8]

Another institution in terms of which political science has very often been sought to be defined is the state. This approach has a very long history. But even in 1928 after reviewing the literature of the definition of politics Garner comes to the conclusion that political science begins and ends with the state.[9] This definition of political science, of course, requires a definition of the state itself. If we cannot define state its role and its area of jurisdiction fairly accurately, we cannot define political science in terms of state. But political scientists seem to have failed to arrive at an agreed definition of state. As Easton points out even if we use the term in the most widely adopted meaning it cannot help us to define political phenomena Because, it excludes "the study of non-literate societies, it stands overshadowed as a tool of analysis by its social utility as a myth; and it constitutes at best a poor formal definition."[10]

6. See, for instance, A.F. Bently, *The Process of Government, op. cit.*, and D.B. Truman. *The Governmental Process* (New York, 1951).
7. Vandyke, *op. cit.*, p. 135.
8. Easton, *op. cit.*, pp. 283.
9. J.W. Garner, *Political Science and Government* (Calcutta, 1952), pp. 7-9.
10. Easton, *The Political System, op. cit.*, pp. 108-9.

Easton very correctly points out that basically the inadequacy of the state concept as a definition of subject matter of political science stems from the fact that it implies that political science is interested in studying a particular kind of institution or organisation of life, not a kind of activity that may express itself through a variety of institutions. He rightly concludes that the institutional criteria of defining political science are not acceptable.

Politics is an activity. Therefore, 'political' must be seen as an activity.[11] It may include the state but it is more than the activities encompassed by this institution. One approach which treats political life as an activity is the power approach. It views political activity as the effort to influence others and to control the behaviour of others. William Robson writes, " it is with power in the society that political science is primarily concerned, its nature, basis, processes, scope and result".[12] Watkins also says, "The proper scope of political science is not the study of the state or of any other specific institutional complex, but the investigation of all associations in so far as they can be shown to exemplify the problem of power".[13] Though the attempt to analyse political life in terms of power emerged as a distinguished approach to the study of politics only recently; yet it could be traced back to the days of Aristotle. Aristotle used the location of power, authority, or rule among the citizens of a political society as a criterion to differentiate one constitution from another. In America the power approach could be traced back to the writings of G.E.G. Catlin. He points out that as a theoretical study, politics is concerned with human relations in association and competition, submission and control. Catlin argues that men seek power in their political negotiations.[14] Catlin's work

11. For a discussion on politics as an activity see H.V. Wiseman, *Politics the Master Science* (London, 1969), pp. 1-5 and 69-86.

12. William A. Robson, *The University Teaching of Social Sciences : Political Science* (Paris, 1954), p. 17.

13. F.M. Watkins, *The State as a Concept of Political Science* (New York, 1934), p. 83.

14. G.E.G. Catlin, *op. cit.*, pp. 210-262.

was immediately followed by a book by Merriam in which he took up the question of political power. He discussed how it originates, accumulates and disintegrates.[15] Lasswell's *Politics Who Gets What, When, How*[16] as Crick says, "is better known than Merriam's *Political Power*; but it is confessedly derived from Merriam's notion of the concept".[17] Hans J. Morgenthau applied the concept of power to the study of international politics.[18] These writings rapidly diffused the idea of power throughout American political science.

The advantage of this approach is that the analysis of political life in terms of power can be applied to any kind of political system—international, national, or local, to groups of various kinds, such as family, kinship groups or Clubs and to historical developments. Political scientists who use the concept of power to identify political activity are of the opinion that political science as an empirical discipline is the study of the shaping and sharing of power.[19] In this approach the purpose of politics comes to be viewed as a pursuit of power. But power is employed to attain some goal and this approach seems to ignore this aspect of the question. Easton rightly says that the power approach fails to identify the boundaries of political science because "power is only one of the significant variables. It omits an equally vital aspect of political life, its orientation towards goals other than power itself".[20]

Easton further points out that this definition of political activity is tco broad. He shows by analysing the writings

15. Char'es E. Merriam, *Political Power: Its Composition and Incidence* (New York, 1934).

16. Harold Lasswell, *Politics Who Gets What, When, How*? (New Yoik, 1936).

17. Crick, *op. cit.*, p. 148.

18. Hans J. Morgenthau, *Politics Among Nations* (New York, 1948).

19. See for Instance H. Lasswell and A. Kaplan, *Power and Society : A Framework of Political Inquiry* (New Heaven, 1950), p. xiv.

20. Easton, *op. cit.*, p. 117.

of Catlin and Lasswell that for the power approach the hierarchical arrangement of relationships within a criminal band or in a respectable paternal club both testify to the existence of political life there. To quote Easton, "The realization of this implication when politics is described as power, pure and simple reveals the excessive breadth of the definition".[21]

He argues that political scientists direct their attention not to power in general but to political power. This view is also supported by Friedrich. While trying to define power and authority Friedrich says that Lasswell's formulation shows that power can, will be and has, indeed, been, a subject that goes a good way beyond the field of politics.[22] This brings us back to the same tricky problem of defining politics. Easton's first objection to the power approach is valid in the sense that power is used for some purposes. As we shall see, later in these pages, power could be seen only in its consequences. The purpose, for which power is used, is therefore of great importance for an understanding of political life. His second objection also holds good because political scientists are not concerned with power relations of all sorts. There, of course, are linkages between political and economic domain in social positions. Politics can't be understood in complete isolation from other social phenomena. But for the purposes of the study of the political life political scientists must focus on the political phenomena. In this sense they are primarily interested in power so far as it plays a role in the political process such a study of power requires a definition of the political process itself. We are then back in square one—the concept power fails to serve as the key to the definition of politics.

Another way of looking at political life as an activity is to describe it as a process of decision making. Decision making

21. *Ibid.*, p. 123.
22. C.J. Friedrich, *An Introduction to Political Theory* (New York, 1967), p. 77.

as a form of analysis could be traced back to the late eighteenth century.[23] Towards the mid-twentieth century it emerged in political science as a variation of the power approach. According to this approach power is important only because it leads to control over the processes through which public decisions are made and executed. In fact this is an approach which stresses that individual and group decision making is the context within which political actions are to be observed.[24] Easton correctly pointed out that this approach had led to the direct interpretation of political life as a set of relationships through which public decisions or policies are formulated and put into effect.[25] He rightly argues that decisions, like power, are characteristic of all other spheres of life as well. Thus, the definition of political science as the study of decision making does not provide guidance in differentiating political decisions from other kinds of decisions. To sum up, in the words of Easton himself,

> Institutional definitions such as government and the state merely serve to define one unknown, political science, by other unknowns. Functional conceptualizations based on power and decision making go well beyond any range of interests that political scientists would at least intuitively seek to embrace within their discipline.[26]

After bringing out the deficiencies of these definitions of politics Easton makes an attempt to give a comprehensive definition of politics. He says that the adequacy of any formal definition will depend on the extent to which it gives a sufficiently general description of the subject matter. So that past and current content areas accepted by most scholars are not excluded or if they are, it is with convincing theoretical

23. See, James, A. Robson, "Decision Making, Political Aspects" in *The International Encyclopedia of Social Sciences*, op. cit., Vol. 4, pp. 55-56,
24. See Cysil Roseman, Charles G. Mayo and F.B. Collinge, *Dimensions of Political Analysis* (New Jersey, 1965), p. 95.
25. Easton, "Political Science" *op. cit.*. p. 284.
26. *Ibid.*, p. 285.

justification.[27] It appears from this that Easton attempts to define political science as what political scientists study. This would be almost a tautology for it immediately necessitates a definition of a political scientist. The problem is how to define a political scientist ? In other words this approach makes us ask the questions—Do we call a discipline political science because a political scientist studies it? Or we call a person a political scientist because he studies political science? Though Easton's approach places him in this unenviable position yet, it is clear that actually he is in search of a definition of politics. This is evident from a paragraph that follows the above statement. In this paragraph he explains that political science can abstract, from all social interactions only those kinds which its theoretical perspectives dictate to be political in nature. Politics, for Easton, is a field of study analytically distinct from other disciplines. But as we will have occasion to note later in these pages the anxiety to conform to the long tradition of political research does affect Easton's view of political life in an adverse manner.

Easton bases his own definition of politics on common sense idea of political life. He holds that the political life includes "an immediate awareness of the pervasiveness of a kind of activity that in our idiom we call politicking"—which actually means "maneuvering for position and power"—which when detected in large social groups is called the struggle for power ; and an activity related in some vague way to problems of government or the making of policy for the whole society in which we live.[28] Such policies are considered to be authoritative for the society. He concludes, "political life concerns all those varieties of activity that influence significantly the kind of authoritative policy adopted for a society and the way it is put into practice".[29] A policy according to Easton, "Consists of a web of decisions and actions that allocate values".[30]

27. *loc. cit.*
28. See, *Ibid.*, p. 127.
29. *Ibid.*, p. 128.
30. *Ibid.*, p. 130.

Policy includes the process of arriving at such a decision and its implementation. The study of policy in his definition includes an examination of the functioning and the determinants of both the legal and the actual policy practices. He is suggesting that political science is concerned with every way in which values are allocated for a society, whether formally enunciated in a law or lodged in the consequences of a practice.[31]

This argument may lead us to a situation where political science will embrace all the spheres of social activity where values are allocated. Easton is aware of this danger. That is why he considers Lasswell's definition of politics far too broad. Lasswell describes political science as "the study of change in the shape and composition of the value patterns of society".[32] To delimit the scope of political science Easton brings in the concept of authority. He specifies that political science is concerned only with authoritative allocation or policies.[33] He suggests that political research is distinctive because it has been trying to reveal the way in which values are affected by authoritative allocations. He is of the opinion that "a policy is authoritative when people to whom it is intended to apply or who are effected by it consider that they must or ought to obey it."[34]

Authoritative allocations are rather common all throughout the social life. Easton is aware of the fact that in organizations that are less than society-wide. we have the existence of a variety of authoritative policies. Easton writes "political science is concerned rather with the relation of the authoritative policies made in such groups as associations, to other kind of policies, those that are considered authoritative for the whole society".[35] Easton, thus, arrives at the conclusion

31. *Ibid.*, p. 131.
32. H. Lasswell, *World Politics and Personal Insecurity* (New York, 1953), p. 3. See also H. Lasswell and A. Kaplan, *op. cit.*, pp. xii & 240.
33. Easton, *The Political System*, *op. cit.*, p. 131.
34. *Ibid.*, p. 132.
35. *Ibid.*, p. 134.

"Political Science is the study of the authoritative allocation of values as it is influenced by the distribution and use of power."[36]

The key terms in this definition, as Easton himself identifies them, are, policy, authority and society. A close look at these terms would reveal that this definition fails to fulfil the task of an adequate definition. The ambiguities of these terms have been very well brought out in an article by Michael Evans.[37] He shows that Easton's concept of policy need not necessarily imply legal or administrative enactments, or indeed consciously formulated decisions at all. Some policy will have legal force much will not. Because for Easton much value-allocation is lodged in the consequences of a practice also. Easton argues in *A Systems Analysis of Political Life* that political response should include modifications in social parameters not in fact generated by the political system but which simply affect the political system.[38] Evans correctly pointed out that we could argue that such modifications might have political effects (for cxample, the invention of mass media) and that these should be investigated by the Political Scientist. But unless it could be shown that the effect was either intentionally produced by the members of the political system or the unintended out come of some activity within the political system it does not seem plausible or even useful to regard all such influence as responses of the political system to stressful conditions. A political system may modify a social parameter or it may have to undergo change as the result of a social modification. We need to distinguish between the two. As Evans rightly says that, Eastons notion of policy has nothing in common with normal usage, and embraces a wide variety of activities, some of which at least should be distinguished. He points out that further, his definition of policy, involving, both

36. *Ibid.*, p. 146.

37. Evrns, *op. cit.*, pp. 117-133.

38. See, David Easton, *A System Analysis of Political Life*, *op. cit.*, pp. 330-1.

intended actions and unintended consequences is in logical conflict with his views on authority relationships.[39]

The second Key term authority is viewed by Easton as a power relationship which is intended in nature.[40] We have already noted that Easton describes an authoritative policy as one which the people to whom it is intended to apply or who are affected by it consider that they must or ought to obey it. Easton does not, therefore, view authority as necessarily legitimate. It could be present both when the legitimacy of the rulers is accepted and where the rulers are obeyed only because they possess a predominance of effective violent sanctions. A quotation from *System Analysis of Political Life* will make this point clear beyond any doubt. He writes,

> Persons in position of political leadership and administration may be able to get others to carry out their intentions simply because on grounds of custom, expediency, self interest or fear it pays the others to do so.[41]

If customs, expediency, self interest or fear could be the basis of authority then Easton's concept of authority cannot be solely dependent on legitimacy.

Easton uses authority to identify political phenomena because he considers it the necessary means of integrating any society. He says, "the fact that the other means of power are

39. Evans, *op. cit.*, p. 125.

40. In a discussion on authority Easton indentifies power relationships (1) manipulation, (2) Persuasion, (3) Force, (4) Authority. In Easton's sense if 'A' sends a message to 'B' and 'B' accepts, the message as the basis of his own behaviour without evaluating it in terms of his own starndards, it is an authority relationship. Easton says "...The fact that in practice he does obey the other is sufficient, evidence for describing the power relationship, as one of authority." See, David Easton, "Perception of authority and political change" in C.J. Friedrich (ed.) *Authority* (Cambridge mass 1958), p. 178.

41. Easton, *A Systems Analysis of Political Life*, *op. cit.*, p. 282.

inadequate, either alone or in combination, for producing the necessary integration of society makes authority itself a necessary means".[42] Easton, of course, does not think that authority itself is a sufficient device for integration of a society. He believes that "In addition to authority probably only force... would be essential for the survival of a society".[43] If in addition to authority Easton considers force as a probable essential condition for the survival of society it poses a problem—considering compliance out of fear (as noted above) as authoritative implies that authority includes force. In this sense Easton appears to have contradicted himself. Because if Authority is considered essential condition for the survival of society and if force is a part of authority then force cannot be considered as another essential condition for survival of society.

However, the above discussion of Easton's use of the term authority shows that he views authority as a necessary condition of integrating society. It is a power relationship and is intentional in nature It is not necessarily dependent on legitimacy. It follows that the authoritative allocation with which the student of politics is concerned must be intentional allocation. Yet by policy, as Evans shows, Easton means not merely consciously formulated plans and intentions but also allocations lodged in the consequences of a practice. Evans points out that Easton's arguments do not establish that authority is pre-eminent over the other relationships, because it is only a necessary condition and not a sufficient condition. He calls Easton's notion of authority "vacuous" because it is not distinguishable from other concepts of similar nature.[44]

If we accept Easton's notion of authority, which is based on compliance, we cannot use this concept to identify political phenomena. Because in this sense obedience or compliance or

42. David Easton, *A Theoretical Approach to Authority* (Standford Clif, 1955), p. 43.

43. *Ibid*, p. 57.

44. Evans, *op. cit.*, pp. 127-28.

at least the feeling that they shall obey becomes the criterion of deciding whether something is political or not. Any allocation or policy which is neither complied to, nor felt that it should be complied to will have to be considered non-political Such an approach will have to treat all those policies and decisions which are not implemented as non-political. But for the purpores of identifying political phenomena, or the subjects of political research such a meaning of policy and decision will create problems. As Frohock says, "we may on occasion wish to view decisions which are 'not' implemented (by either enforcement or acceptance) as quite political".[45] Frohock mentions two ways of over coming this difficulty ; but he himself has found these unsatisfactory. First, we can exclude from the category of the political all decisions which people do not feel they ought to obey for one reason or another. But this will amount to assuming that there is a near unanimity about political decisions. Which in turn brings in a consensus bias. Secondly, authoritative policy may be considered as legitimate regardless of whether or not the members of a society feel at any given moment that they ought to obey it. But this begs the question how can authoritative policy be legitimate if the members of a society do not feel that they ought to obey it ?.

Almond and Coleman seem to have adopted the second approach when they defined the political system as a system of interactions performing the functions of integration and adaptation by means of employment, or threat of employment, of more or less legitimate physical compulsions.[46] This reminds us of Weber's approach to the problem. These scholars have not really gone far beyond Weber's definition of state as "a human community that 'successfully' claims the monopoly of the legitimate use of physical force within a

45. F.M. Frohock. *The Nature of Political Inquiry*, *op. cit.*, pp. 89-90.

46. G. Almond and J. Coleman ; *Politics of Developing Area*, (Princeton, New Jersey 1960), pp. 3-64.

given territory".[47] Force, for Weber, could either be legitimate or illegitimate, the legitimate force was called 'authority'. He tried to conceptualize the political phenomena by focusing on the events which participate in the exercise of ultimate force.[48] But as Frohock shows, the idea of ultimate force is close to the dead concept of sovereignty. Moreover, this will again drag the political scientist to the unnecessary debate over the distinction between power and authority.[49] It is, thus, clear that Easton's notion of authority cannot help us to arrive at an acceptable definition of politics.

The third important concept in his definition of politics is society. His idea of political would include only those phenomena which are related to the "societal" political system. This becomes clear from the distinction he draws between political and para-political systems. Para-political systems are aspects only of sub-systems in a society. They are sub-systems of sub-systems. Easton identifies para-political systems as internal systems of groups and organization. He chooses not to consider them co-ordinate with the more inclusive political system of a society, because "para-political systems are concerned only with problems of authoritative allocations within the groups".[50]

The societal political system, according to Easton, has three components : the authorities, the regime and the political community. The political community consists of a group of persons bound together by a "political division of labour". In a later chapter when we examine his idea of the political system we shall discuss these components in details. Here it suffices to say that he views political community as one the

47. Max Weber, 'Politics as a vocation' in H H. Gerth and C. Wright Mills (eds) *From Max Weber, Essays in Sociology* (London 1948), p. 78.

48. Max Weber, *The Theory of Social and Economic Organisation*, (Illinois, 1964), p. 322.

49. Frohock, *op. cit.*, p. 91.

50. Easton, *A Framework of Political Analysis*, *op. cit.*, p. 55.

scope of which varies with the scope of the political system under study. To quote Easton, "for a person to say that he is a parisian, a Frenchman and a European indicates three different levels of political community to which he simultaneously adheres".[51] In this sense the members of the political community, in Eastonian scheme of things may each come from a quite different society. They don't need to have a common cultural background. Like his political system his idea of a society is also "constructive", i.e., constructed by the scholar for the purposes of analysis. As Evans points out :

> On the constructivist view this is perfectly sound. The society, of which the political community is itself an aspect of that society's political sub-system, would be some wider set of variables selected by the observer for description and explanation. On this view, Easton's claim that the authoritative allocations which concern the political scientist are those for a society as a whole simply follows by definition.[52]

We have already noted that he excludes para-political systems from the scope of political science because authoritative allocations in such systems do not effect the whole society. He, however, does not give us any theoretical reason for doing so. He merely says that these are only aspects of sub-systems in a society. Then he goes on to say :

> The decision to confine the analysis to political systems has the added virtue that without sacrificing theoretical criteria of selection, it conforms to a long tradition of political research. This has dictated that the subject matter of political research, at its most general level and broadest context should embrace the most inclusive political system of a society.[53]

51. Easton, *A Systems Analysis of Political Life*, *op. cit.* pp. 171-72.
52. Evans, *op. cit.*, p. 128.
53. Easton, *A Framework of Political Analysis*, *op. cit.*, p. 55.

One wonders why Easton must conform to this "Long tradition of political research ?" This tradition centres round the concept of state and Easton himself has successfully brought out the difficulties associated with the state concept. Moreover, a good definition of politics should be able to identify political phenomena so that we can delimit our field of study. If such a definition brings in even some traditionally non-political phenomena within the scope of politics that should not disqualify such a definition. A definition should be judged by its own merits and not by the fact of its conforming or not conforming to one or the other tradition.

It is thus clear that the key concepts in Easton's definition are ambiguous. Evans has legitimately concluded that Easton has not defined the term political and has therefore made no distinction between the political and the non-political.[54] Vandyke also holds a similar opinion. He maintains that Easton's definition is an improvement on Lasswells definition of politics as the study of changes in the shape and composition of the value patterns of society ; but even here the key words are difficult to define, or are so broad in their application that they are of dubious help in identifying the political.[55]

Though Easton's definition does not serve the important and declared task of distinguishing political phenomena from non-political phenomena ; yet it seems to have served another purpose, and altogether different one. This purpose concerns the level of political research and consequently the types of questions a political scientist is expected to ask. We have seen that his definition emphasises the allocation of values. As a result his political science becomes the study of how 'values' are authoritatively allocated in the society. As Mitchel says, "this allocative framework is in many ways analogous to the

54. Evans, *op. cit.*, p. 129.

55. Vandyke, *op. cti.*, pp. 145-46.

theories of income distribution and the allocation of resources in economics."[56]

In Economics William Stanely Jevons was one of the early propagators of the allocative framework. As Keynes pointed out Jevons was alarmed and excited by the idea of the exhaustion of resource.[57] He visualized the problem of allocation of resources as fundamental to economics. The problem with which Jevons thought economics ought to be mainly concerned was how to allocate a given set of resources among competing uses so that a given set of desires would be most effectively satisfied.[53] If this view is accepted then the boundaries of the subject are fixed around the market. The system of economic variables and their area of determination is virtually identified with the market or with the set of interconnected markets that constitute the sphere of exchange. Thus economics of this kind enables the economists to confine their analysis to the distribution process without going into the sphere of production. On the other hand, economists like Ricardo and Marx view production as fundamental to the study of economics. In a beautiful passage Marx pointed out that one must begin with production and that study of distribution without linking it with production is futile. He writes :

> Hunger is hunger ; but the hunger that is satisfied by cooked meat eaten with knife and fork differs from hunger that devours raw meat with the help of hands, nails and teeth. Production thus produces not only the object of consumption but also the mode of consumption, not only objectively but also subjectively. Production therefore, creates the consumer.[59]

56. W.C. Mitchell, "Politics as The Allocation of Values : A Critique", *Ethics*, Vol. LXXI (Jan 1963) No. 2, p. 79.
57. J.M. Keynes, "William Stanely Jevons : 1835-1882" *Journal of Royal Statistical Society*, Part III (1936), p. 522.
58. Ronald E. Meek. *Studies in the Labour Theory of Value*, (New York, and London, 1956), p. 248.
59. Karl Marx. *A Contribution to the Critique of Political Economy* (Moscow, 1970), p. 197.

Marx then goes on to argue that production produces consumption : (1) by providing the material of consumption ; (2) by determining the mode of consumption ; (3) by creating in the consumer a need for the objects which it first presents as products. It, therefore, produces the object and the mode of consumption and the urge to consume. Marx further argues that similarly, consumption produces the predisposition of the producer by posing him as a purposive requirement. Consumption is only a phase of production. Therefore, production is fundamental to the study of economics.

The distributive or allocative theories, mainly identified with the neo-classical marginalist school of economic thought completely reject the idea that the economic system could be properly understood only and only if one starts with the relations of production peculiar to the particular mode of production under consideration. These theories emphasize the study of distribution, but distribution determines the individual's share in the world of products on the basis of social laws. It intervenes between the producer and the product, i.e., production and consumption. Therefore, distribution is not an independent sector along side and outside production. Both are closely linked.[60]

However, the neo-classical distribution and allocative theorists in economics confine their attention to the distributive process and reduce the problem of distribution to the pricing of requisite inputs by a market process which simultaneously determines the inter-connected system of out puts and inputs. As Economics of this kind does not enquire into the question of production, such a question as the origins of surplus could not even be raised within the stated terms of economic analysis. As Dobb shows, such a question will be considered meaningless or as falling outside the boundaries of the subject.[61] If the question of surplus is not raised one cannot ask questions of property ownership or class-relations and conflict.

60. *Ibid.*, p. 199.
61. See, Maurice Dobb, *Theories of value and Distribution since Adam Smith* (London, New York, Melbourn, 1977), pp. 167-210.

Similarities between Easton's approach to political science and this kind of economic analysis are obvious. Like Jevons Easton also starts with scarcity and alternative uses of scarce resources. He makes it clear when he says :

> It is patent that without the provision for some means of deciding among competing claims to limited values, society would be rent by constant strife; the regularised interaction which distinguish a society from a random mob of individuals could not exist. Every society provides some mechanisms, however rudimentary they may be, for authoritively resolving differences about the ends that are to be pursued, that is, for deciding who is to get what there is of the desirable things. An authoritative allocation of values is unavoidable.[62]

Easton then assumes that authoritative allocation or politics becomes necessary in a society as a result of the inherent scarcity and the possibility of alternative uses of such scarce resources. In an article already referred to Mitchell shows that such a position involves five assumptions similar to those in allocative theories of eeonomics. These are : (1) that resources available to a society are limited; (2) that limited resources may have alternative uses; (3) that men strive for different and conflicting ends; (4) that man is rational; and (5) that he is motivated to maximise his returns.[63]

The validity of these assumptions as Mitchell shows could be questioned. Though he expresses his reservations about the validity of these assumptions yet he does not examine the consequences of adopting such an approach. The point which we want to emphasize is that by opting for an allocative approach, political scientists, like allocative economists, shift

62. Easton, *The Political System, op. cit.*, p. 137. In his interview with the present author Easton reiterates this point by claims contrary to our interpretation that his analysis shares the same promises as those of Hobbes and Karl Marx. See, Appendix.

63. Mitchell, *op. cit.*, pp. 79-87.

the focus of the discipline to a plane where it is no more necessary for them to investigate the questions related to the sources of political power. The distribution and use of power is important. They do effect the allocation of values. But if we want to understand the political life we must also ask why power is distributed in a particular manner. But like the allocative economists allocative political scientists also prevent the discipline from asking such fundamental questions.

As we have noted earlier in economics distributive processes comprising the allocation and consumption are closely related to production. In fact production determines their nature. This is not to rule out the fact that once produced such processes also influence the production. In the same way allocation of values and distribution and use of power in politics are closely linked to the sources and determinants of political power. Though like in economics here, too, these processes may in turn influence the sources of power. The allocative theories in both the disciplines do not go into the cores, i.e., the production in economics and the determinants and sources of power in politics. We have already noted the consequences of such an approach in economics. Let us now examine whether Easton's approach to political science also produces similar consequences.

While discussing his definition of politics we have noted that he defines political science as the study of the authoritative allocation of values as it is influenced *by the distribution and use of power*.[64] Here in fairness to Easton it must be stated that his focus is not merely on the allocation of values, it is on the distribution and use of power also. Even at the risk of digression we must also take note of his assertion that his political science does not confine itself merely to the allocative aspects of political system. He says that the question that confronts political theory is—how does a system can persist

64. Easton, *The Political System*, *op. cit.*, p. 146.

long enough to continue to make decisions about allocation of values.[65]

But even when Easton proposes to examine how a system persists he actually proposes to examine only how the decisions regarding allocation of values enable the system to persist. It is rather intriguing to note that while trying to formulate a theory of system persistence Easton does not feel the necessity of looking into the nature and determinants of political power and therefore to the nature of the system itself. He seems to believe that an examination of the way in which policy decisions (outputs) effect the members and how these effects generate support and demand (inputs for the system) would enable us to understand how a system persists? Easton draws our attention to the continuous flow of information about the effects of 'outputs' on the members through a feed back system. He says that this enables the authorities to adjust their behaviour to meet the needs of the system. He then concludes that "it is the fact that there can be such a continuous flow of effects and information between system and environment,... that ultimately accounts for the capacity of a political system to persist in a world even of violently fluctuating changes".[66] Persistence in Eastons use of the term means the continuity of the process of authoritative allocation of the values.

His very definition of politics, as the authoritative allocation of values as influenced by the distribution and use of power fixes the boundary of the discipline in a manner that the political scientist is required to examine only how the distribution and use of power effect the allocation of values. Power itself is considered as given. Such an approach does not require them to examine the determinants and the nature of power. But distribution of power would always be effected or influenced by the determinants of power itself. The nature of the

65. Easton, *A Systems Analysis of Political Life*, *op. cit.*, p. 31.
66. *Ibid.*, p. 32.

allocation of values in a feudal monarchy will be different from that of a bourgeois democracy. This difference is the effect of the difference in the distribution and use of power. But even this difference in the distribution and use of power is the result of the basic difference in the determinants of power. Unless we understand the various nature of these determinants we cannot understand the political life. In fact if we do not study this aspect of the question our study of the political system will remain confined to the existing power relations which are considered as given. This kind of analysis also views the values as given. But values like political system themselves are transitional in nature. To understand this transitional nature of the values, and therefore of their allocations, we must understand the transitional distribution and use of power. To paraphrase Marx—power is power but the power of a tribal chief is different from that of the executive head of a bourgeois democracy. As production determines distribution in economics in politics also the determinants of power shapes the distribution and use of power which in turn effects the allocation of values. To understand politics, therefore, we must understand what determines power in the political system under study and how?

Power itself is an abstract term and there is no universally acceptable definition of power. But in all situations of power, "the notion of a capacity to determine events and conditions is involved."[67] Power is visible only through its consequences. They are the proofs of existence of power. The inequalities of wealth, income and welfare that divide the population are among the most crucial of such consequences. They are the most visible manifestations of division of power in a society.

It is possible for the allocationists to argue that even these inequalities are the results of the decisions taken to that effect and therefore the central problem of political science is to understand how these decisions are made. This would in

67. J. Westergaard and H. Resler, *State in the Capitalist Society*, (Harmondsworth, 1976), p. 142.

fact bring us back to the question of allocation of values. But as Steven Lukes shows political power which effects such inequalities is not to be seen only in positive decisions. In a penetrating study of power[68] he discusses different views on power. He divides these into three—one dimensional, two dimensional and three dimensional views. The one dimensional, view, according to him involves a focus on behaviour in the making of decisions or issues over which there is an observable conflict of interests seen as express policy preferences revealed by political participation. The two dimensional view of power, on the other hand, allows for consideration of the ways in which decisions are prevented from being taken on political issues over which there in an observable conflict of interests seen as embodied in express policy preferences and sub-political grievances. But Lukes points out that both these approaches follow in the steps of Max Weber for whom power was the probability of 'individuals realizing their will's despite resistance of others, whereas power to control the agenda of politics and exclude political issues cannot be adequately analysed unless it is seen as a function of collective forces and social arrangements It is clear that these two approaches to power believe that an actual conflict is always present in any power relationship. But two types of power, manipulation and authority may not involve such conflict. If we assume that power is exercised only when a conflict is present we obviously ignore the most effective use of power. Power not only settles conflicts one way or the other, it also prevents them from arising. This is the most effective use of power. This might of course give the impression that this kind of power exists when there are grievances but those are denied entry into the political process and as a result conflicts do not arise. But the most significant use of power is to prevent people from having grievances in such a manner that they accept their role in the existing order of things. This is very often called the process of political socialization which is defined as the process by which political cultures are main-

68. Steven Lukes, *Power : A Radical View* (London, 1976).

tained and changed. If a particular political culture fails to create a situation, when people by and large accept their roles in the existing order, the political culture and therefore the political system, of which this political culture is a part, it will fail to maintain itself. This task of making people '*accept*' their role in the existing order of things is fulfilled by what Ralph Miliband calls, "shaping of the consciousness".[69] This process contributes to the stabilization and legitimization of the system. The ideas which do this trick of shaping the consciousness are the ideas of the ruling class.

With the help of the ideas, which become dominant as a result of their own dominant position, the ruling classes try to run the society in a manner which does not permit even the emergence of grievances. Althusser has shown that this is achieved through "the ideological state apparatuses"[70] when Gramsci talked of hegemony he had this process in his mind. The idea is that the ruling classes do persuade the other classes to accept its own moral, political and cultural values.[71] The ruling classes do not always use brutal force to maintain its rule over the rest of the society. They have subtle methods of preventing people from articulating and even realizing their own grievances.

A proper understanding of political power, therefore, requires an examination of this process also. We must examine the various ways in which political issues are kept out of politics. Such ways may include operation of social forces, institutional practice or individuals decisions. The inequali-

69. Ralph Miliband, *Marxism and Politics*, (Oxford, 1977), pp. 42-65.

70. L. Althusser, "Ideology and ideological state apparatuses" in B.R. Cosin (ed.) *Educational Structure and Society* (Harmondsworth, 1972), pp. 242-280.

71. A. Gramsci, in Quintin Hoare and Geoffrey Nowell (eds.) *Selections from the Prison Note Books*, (New York, 1971), p. 161.

ties created by power are not to be seen as results of concrete decisions. These very often are the results of certain social mechanisms, principles and assumptions. These do favour the interest of one or the other group vis-a-vis the rest of the population. In a capitalist society for instance, the primary assumptions of this nature are private property and market. In such a society the idea based on these assumptions are diffused in such a manner that a large section of the population tend to accept the resultant inequalities as legitimate. This is the most significant use of political power. "Power", to quote Westergaard and Resler, "is to be found more in uneventful routine than in conscious and active exercise of will".[72]

The distribution and use of power in any society is directly related to such 'uneventful routine' which operates on the basis of the prevailing assumptions. The authoritative allocation of values in any society, in the ultimate analysis, would also be determined by these assumptions. Power, in this sense, and the nature of its determinants are therefore central to political science. For Easton, however, Power is only of derivative interest the focus of his political science is mainly on allocation of values.[73] But as Gramsci says, "The first element (of politics) is that there really do exist rulers and ruled, leaders and led".[74] The rulers can't rule and leaders cannot lead unless they exercise power.

Moreover, Easton's view of power does not allow the examination of the crucial assumption through which political power is used in the most significant way. His approach requires a political scientist to take note of power only where authoritative allocations were involved. Allocations involve decisions. Therefore, his view of power centres round the

72. Westergaard and Resler, *op. cit.*, p. 144.

73. Easton, *The Political System, op. cit.*, p. 143.

74. Gramsci, *op. cit.*, p. 144.

concept of decision. We have already seen that this amounts to taking an one dimensional view of power.

Power could be studied at two different levels. At one level the questions concerned 'core assumptions'. What are the implicit terms of reference within which conflict about policy is confined for all practical purposes; which excludes alternatives outside that range from consideration? Whose and what interest do the core assumptions favour? At a lower level the questions concern the conflict and outcome of pressures within the boundaries set by the core assumptions.[75]

Under Easton's definition of politics the study of power will be confined to the lower level. As it concerns itself with issues related to policy decisions or allocation of values it will never question the 'Core assumptions'. Macpherson shows that the current empirical theorists view political power as power over others ; but they do not go into its extractive nature in any unequal society. He maintains that at the most they ask questions like – how power holders recruit power ? What are the conditions for the maintenance of a stable system of inputs to and output from political power ?[76] For Easton, of course, it is not necessary to go into the determinants of power. His definition of politics delimits the fieid of political inquiry in a manner that he does not have to go into the 'Core assumptions'. Once political phenomena is defined in terms of allocation or distribution such questions as to the purpose of political power and its determinants do not any more fall within the jurisdiction of political science. Such an approach render's political science a merely descriptive discipline. In the case of Easton, of course, such an approach fits into his scheme of formulating a conceptual framework which he calls a political theory. Easton's definition, thus prevents his political science from examining the roots and the purpose of political power,

75. Westergaard and Resler, *op. cit.*, p. 248.

76. C.B. Macpherson: *Democratic Theory*, (Oxford, 1973), pp. 39-47.

in the political system understudy. This puts him squarely in line with Jevon's. Both of them delimit the scope of their discipline in a manner which puts these questions beyond the boundaries of the respective disciplines. In this sense Easton seems to have brought a Javonian revolution in political science.

CHAPTER 5

A Model of Political System : An Exercise in Futility

The concept of Political System occupies the Central Position in Easton's Political Science and his view of Political Theory. In all his works this concept remains the major point of focus. In fact it is this concept of political system in which he pins his hope for developing an empirical theory of politics. As early as 1953 in his book *The Political System*,[1] Easton used the term political system and pleaded for adoption of a systems approach to the study of political life, but he was not able as yet to build a proper framework for the study of political life. It was only in his later works that Easton tries to develop a framework for analysis of political life within the systems frame. In a paper published in 1957[2] he tried to draw the outline of his framework. In 1965 Easton published two major books[3] on this theme. These books give a detailed contour of his idea of the political system.

1. Easton, *The Political System, op. cit.*
2. Easton, "An Approach to the Analysis of Political System : in Stephen V. Mosma and Jack. R. Vander Silk (eds.), *American Politics : Research and Readings*, (New York, 1970), pp. 5-18. This paper was originally published in *World Politics* Vol. IX (April 1957), pp. 383-400.
3. Easton, *A Framework of Political Analysis, op. cit.*, and *Systems Analysis of Political Life, op. cit.*

Easton points out that political scientists have been trying to develop concepts to describe the most obvious and encompassing properties of politics. According to him, "the idea of political system proves to be an appropriate and indeed unavoidable starting point in this search".[4] Students of political life, assume that the phenomena of politics tend to cohere and to be mutually related. There are certain kinds of activities which are closely related to what may be called political life. The elements of political activity, such as governmental organizations, pressure groups, voting, parties, and the social elements related to these such as classes, regional groupings and so forth, all show close interactions. Easton admits that these elements are, part of the whole social process and therefore are parts of analytical systems other than the political. But he argues that, they show a marked political relevance more than purely accidental or random. He suggests that "the elements of political life have some form of determinate relation. The task of research is to discover what these are. *In short, political life constitutes a concrete political system which is an aspect of the whole social system.*[5] (emphasis added)

It is, therefore, clear that Easton proposes to view political life as a system which is viewed as a part of the whole social system. He does not think that this can be delinked from the social system. But he considers it possible and even necessary to set it temporarily apart for purposes of analysis. He, of course, recognizes that all social life is inter-dependent and as a result it is artificial to isolate any set of social relations from the whole for special attention. But this artificiality, according to him, is imposed upon political scientists by the need for 'simplification' of their data. He says that political science is compelled to abstract from the whole social system some variables which seem to cohere more closely than others. He cites the example of economics where, price, supply, demand and choice among wants are looked upon as a sub-system which

4. Easton, *The Political System, op. cit.*, p. 96.
5. *Ibid.*, p. 97.

can be profitably examined, temporarily, apart from the whole social system. In political science the analytica tool for this purpose is a theoretical construct conceptualizing a political system. He says, "... it consists first, of a set of concepts corresponding to the important political variables and, second of statements about the relations among these concepts."[6]

This point becomes clear from his views about the social system. Basically, Easton puts in a system language what is generally accepted among social scientists, i.e., that the society consists of various aspects of life. Easton shows that over the course of time it has appeared useful to identify different kinds of interactions prevalent in the social life. He is of the opinion that, since various subsystems of the social system do not represent the totality of the interactions involved in a society, but only parts of them that have been abstracted out of the apperceptive mass of behaviours "these systems are analytic in character. Political interactions constitute one kind of such systems".[7]

This analytic system is a unit of analysis. Evans rightly describes this system as one hypothetically "constructed by the observer."[8] Easton is of the opinion that a system could be either "natural" or "constructive". A natural system is one in which a set of interactions naturally coheres. But he holds that the idea of natural system can serve little useful theoretical purpose because "this would in no way help us to locate such systems. We would still have the task of taking any set of political relationships and exploring their connectedness".[9] Easton clearly states that the search for natural systems would create a virtually insurmountable difficulty by opening the door to interminable dispute on as to whether or not a set of activities 'really' forms a system. Easton rightly argues that

6. *Ibid.*, p. 98.

7. Easton : *A Framework of Political Analysis, op. cit.* p. 38.

8. Evans, *op. cit.*, p. 119.

9. Easton, *A Framework of Political Analysis, op. cit.*, p. 29.

we shall find this dispute to be totally unnecessary, spacious and distracting issue.[10]

Easton further points out that, it leaves open the question as to whether the existence of what is only an apparent interdependence would thereby transform the elements into a system of some kind. He shows that if we accept the concept of natural system it would be necessary to demonstrate that the relationships among variables are relevant for an understanding of the operation of the system. He concludes, "It would still leave us saddled with the crucial problem of establishing the interconnectedness of a set of variables and demonstrating their theoretical relevance or meaningfulness."[11]

In the face of such difficulties in viewing political life as a natural system, Easton postulates that any set of variables selected for description and explanation may be considered a system of behaviour. He believes that this will simplify the problems of analysis enormously. This is what he calls a 'constructive system'. Stating the advantages of this approach Easton says that "It avoids and eliminates all possible disputes about whether or not the object of our analysis is or is 'really' not a system.... It enables us to say that one that was totally uninteresting because we could see very little inter-relationship among its parts has suddenly become significant, new data having suggested possible connection."[12]

In this approach, the only thing that commands our attention is whether a particular set of activities is an interesting one, in the sense that it is relevant and helps us to understand some theoretical problems, or whether it is worthless or trivial from this point of view. Easton hopes that such an approach will save the political scientist the trouble of deciding which is really a system and which is not. But it introduces an equally ticklish problem of deciding whether a set of variables is inte-

10. *Ibid.*, p. 30.
11. *Loc. cit.*
12. *Ibid.*, p. 31.

resting or not. To paraphrase Easton himself, it would still leave us saddled with the crucial problem of establishing the interesting character of a set of variables by demonstrating their theoretical relevance or meaningfulness.[13] It is, therefore, clear that Easton's claim that the 'constructive system' simplifies the problem of analysis is not tenable.

However, Easton builds up his systems analysis around this concept of the analytical political system. The general premises of this analysis are :

1. System : It is useful to view political life as a system of behaviour.

2. Environment : A system is distinguishable from the environment in which it exists and open to influences from it.

3. Response : Variations in the structures and processes within a system may usefully be interpreted as constructive or positive alternative efforts by members of a system to regulate or cope with stress flowing from environmental as well as internal sources.

4. Feedback : The capacity of a system to persist in the face of stress is a function of the presence and nature of information and other influences that return to its actors or decision makers.[14]

By the time Easton stated the general premises of his analysis some other political scientists also had developed approaches which interpret political life as a system of behaviour. Easton claims that the third and the fourth of these premises fundamentally distinguish his kind of systems analysis from the

13. *Ibid.*, p. 30.

14. *Ibid.*, pp. 24-25.
See, also David Easton, 'Systems Analysis in Politics and its Critics', *Hogaku Kenkyu*, 45, (Tokyo, 1972) pp. 41-70.

other systems approaches to the study of political life. Almond and Coleman developed a model for a comparative study of political systems.[15] They attribute three major properties to the interactions which form the system. These are (1) Comprehensiveness ; (2) Interdependence ; and (3) existence of boundaries.[16] Their idea of the political system of course does not have the properties of response and feedback. In this sense Easton's concept of system is distinguishable from the Almond and Coleman model. But Easton's claim that these two premises give his approach an unique position in political science is not maintainable because Karl Deutsch's approach seems to have used both of these concepts. Deutsch borrows his model from cybernatics—the theory of information, self-regulating machines, computers, and the physiology of the nervous system. A cybernatic system recognizes stimuli. It learns, adjusts itself automatically upon receiving feedback about its performance, and moves through a determined number of possible states. Karl Deutsch applies this model to describe a political system. Deutsch thus uses the concepts of response and feedback in his model.[17]

However, Easton conceives political life "as a boundary maintaining set of interactions imbedded in and surrounded by other social systems to the influence of which it is constantly exposed".[18] He explains that this concept of system may mean either empirical or symbolic systems. In the empirical sense it refers to the empirical behaviour of the political life. In the symbolic sense it refers to the set of symbols through which the behaviour of the empirical system could be identified, described, determined or explained. He proposes to deal with the empirical or behaving system with respect to which

15. Gabriel A. Almond, James S. Coleman (eds.) *The Politics of the Developing Areas*, *op. cit.*, pp. 3-64.

16. *Ibid.*, p. 7.

17. Karl W. Deutsch, *The Nerves of Government: Models of Political Communication and Control* (New York, 1963), pp. 80-85.

18. Easton, *A Framework of Political Analysis*, *op. cit.*, p. 25.

he seeks to develop a theoretical construct. This theoretical construct is designated a political system. This approach views the political system as one that is capable of regulating its own behaviour through its internal mechanism which is at its disposal. Easton's political system is a goal setting, self-transforming and creatively adaptive system consisting of human beings who are capable of anticipating, evaluating and acting constructively to prevent disturbances in the environment.[19]

It appears that Easton has given a free hand to the members of the political system to deal with disturbances. It is true that the members of a political system may take steps to prevent disturbances ; but they can act only within a particular range. We shall see during the course of our discussion that the members of the system, and in that sense the system itself, are not free to act in this manner to enable themselves to deal with disturbances.

These disturbances create stress on the system. Stress actually means pressure on the essential variables of the system. Easton holds that all political systems have two essential variables—"the capacity of the system to allocate values for the society and ensure their acceptance".[20] If it becomes impossible for the system to arrive at political decisions, or, if after making such decisions it fails to make these accepted, it will not be able to function. Evans has rightly pointed out that the two variables are really one, for the only criterion Easton offers for allocations being authoritative is their being accepted.[21] A political system refers to authoritative allocations only. It is clear from our discussion of Easton's definition of politics, in the preceding chapter, that if allocations are made but those are not accepted by the populace or at least considered obligatory, they are not authoritative and, therefore, not political. Such allocations in fact will not fall within the boundaries of the political system. Easton is mistaken in con-

19. *Ibid.*, p. 132.
20. *Ibid.*, p. 96.
21. Evans, *op. cit.*, p. 132 FN 22.

sidering the allocations and ensuring their acceptance as two variables. In the context of the political system all allocation will have to be authoritative and therefore, ensuring their acceptance is inherent to political allocations themselves that is if we accept Easton's definition of politics. There is actually one essential variable and that is authoritative allocation of values. For the purpose of this discussion, however, we shall continue to refer to them as two variables as Easton himself does.

Easton explains that as a result of the stress pouring in from the environment of the system these variables may be pushed beyond the critical range. The concept of environment takes us to the issue of boundaries. Easton begins his discussion of the boundaries of the political system by pointing out that "political research seeks first and foremost to understand the way in which values are authoritatively allocated, not for a group within the society but for the whole society."[22] That is why it becomes necessary to distinguish between what Easton calls the "political system" or "Societal Political System" and the "Para-Political System". Political systems are sub-systems of the social systems. The Para-Political systems are aspects of sub-systems in a society. He argues that the members of para-political systems neither accept nor are expected to accept the responsibilities for dealing with the major problems generated by the fact that an aggregate of persons live together as a society, share some aspects of life and are compelled, thereby, to try to resolve their differences together. These responsibilities transcend the scope of any single organised group. Para-political systems are concerned only with problems of authoritative allocations within the group.[23] These responsibilities are undertaken by political systems. He says, "The societal political system...possesses a range of responsibilities that are far broader in scope than those of the para-political systems within the small groups of a society".[24] Easton

22. Easton, *The Political System, op. cit.*, p. 134.

23. Easton, *A Framework of Political Analysis, op. cit.*, p. 52.

24. *Ibid.*, p. 53.

points out that the powers enjoyed by the two kinds of political systems also vary according to their responsibilities. The power available to the Societal Political system for attempting to regulate differences are usually broader, corresponding thereby to its greater range of responsibilities.[25]

Easton, thus distinguishes the political system from para-political systems on the basis of the wider responsibilities it bears and the wider range of corresponding powers it exercises. Having distinguished the political and the para-political systems he goes on to identify the basic structural units of analysis in the political system. The political system reflects one aspect of the total interactions of the biological persons in a society. These persons, as they engage in political interactions of one sort or another, are referred to as members. This term identifies the general role of a person in a given society with respect to political life. Member is an analytical category. The societal political system comprising such members is placed in an environment. Easton shows that in the case of physical or biological systems the boundaries are simple enough to perceive.[26] They form the spatial or material limits to the collection of variables in which we are interested. With the examples of the apple, the human body, the boulder, the waterfalls and the solar system he shows that these variables could be seen clearly or it needs very little imagination to perceive them. Easton points out that the identification of such boundaries in the case of political systems is not as simple as it appears to be because a system of social interactions, is normally so diffused throughout a society that we have considerable difficulty in accommodating the same imagery to these actions, taken collectively, that we apply so easily to physical and biological system.[27] Easton maintains that boundaries are, in fact, not phenomenally out there waiting to be identified. They conform to our general conclusion about the character of systems, that they are products of analytic selection..."[28]

25. *Ibid.*, pp. 53-54.
26. *Ibid.*, pp. 63-64.
27. *Ibid.*, p. 64.
28. *Ibid.*, p. 65.

In this sense geo-political boundaries of society do not help us to identify the boundaries of a political system. In fact in their theoretical status boundaries need not always be spatial in nature. "Analytically the boundaries of all systems may be interpreted as the criteria of inclusion in or exclusion from the system forming the focus of interest".[29] Thus boundaries like systems, in Easton's sense of the term, are purely analytical. But while the system may be an intellectual construct in practice this construct can be seen only in a spatial context. For instance when we speak of the Indian political system we cannot avoid referring to the geopolitical boundaries within which this system operates. In this sense, the empirical aspects of the boundaries of a political system cannot be ignored. Though Easton suggests that boundaries are not empirical he holds that there are empirical indicators of these boundaries. The key to these indicators, according to Easton, is the structural differentiation. The more differentiated the structures in a society are, the clearer are these indicators. He says that the clarity of the boundary between the political system and other social systems is signalized by the following properties. (1) The extent of distinction of political roles and activities from other roles and activities, or conversely the extent to which they are all imbedded in united structures such as the family or kinship groups, (2) the extent to which occupants of roles form a separate group in the society and possess a sense of internal solidarity and cohesion, (3) the extent to which political roles take shape of a hierarchy which is distinguishable from other hierarchies based upon wealth, prestige or other non-political criteria ; and (4) the extent to which the recruitment process and criteria of selection differ for the occupants of political as contrasted with other roles.[30]

Easton then goes on to describe the environment of the political system. The environment of the political system embraces the social as well as the physical environment. This environment is composed of two basically different types of

29. *Ibid.*, p. 68.
30. *Ibid.*, p. 69.

systems, intra-societal and extra-societal. The intra-societal systems in the environment of political system are those which lie outside the boundaries of a political system and yet within the same society. Easton divides these intra-societal systems, falling outside the boundaries of political system, into the ecological, biological, personality and social systems. Social systems are further sub-divided into cultural, social-structural, economic and demographic.[31]

There are systems outside the society of which the political system itself is a social sub-system. These may have important consequences for the persistence or change of a political system.[32] Easton suggests that we view the whole international society as an unit external to any given political systems.[33] Like the intra-societal environment this extra-societal environment also has its own sub-systems like an international ecological system, international political system, and such international social systems as an international culture, international economy and international demographic system.[34]

Easton, thus, conceives two distinct environments of the political systems, the intra-societal and the extra-societal. While the intra-societal environment is composed of sub-systems of a society which fall outside the political sub-system of that society, the extra-societal environment is the international society. It comprises the sub-systems of the international society. Recognition of this fact poses a problem for any one who wants to use Easton's framework. The extra-societal and the intra-societal environments have the same categories of sub-systems, i.e., cultural, economic and demographic sub-systems. The national parts of these sub-systems are inseparable parts of the international system. Therefore, one part of them cannot be placed in the intra-societal environment while the other is placed in the extra-societal

31. *Ibid.*, pp. 71-73.
32. *Ibid.*, p. 73.
33. *Ibid.*, p. 74.
34. *Loc. cit.*

environment. For instance, if we try to examine the American Political system within Easton's framework, we are expected to place the American Economy in the intra-societal environment and the international economy in the extra-societal environment. But under Easton's scheme as we tried to explain above the American economy is also a sub-system of the International economic system and as such falls in the extra-societal environment of the American political system. Even as a theoretical construct it will be impossible to place the same sub-system in both the environments, specially when in Easton's framework, there is no flow of inputs from the extra-societal to intra-societal environment.[35] Easton's model aims at simplifying political data; but the intra-societal and the extra-societal environments in his framework overlap in such a manner that instead of simplifying political data it will add to the existing confusion.

Easton's political system is an open and responding system. It is an open system because, "it is a system imbedded in an environment and exposed to what happens there." It is a responding system because it "constitutes a set of behaviours through which positive action may be taken to cope with the influences operating on it".[36] Such influences may at times become stressful, but the system does not collapse under such conditions. It is expected to respond in a manner so that the system can survive. The capacity to respond to stress is a remarkable feature of Easton's framework. He claims that what distinguishes his systems theory is that it presents a view of political life as a responding system [37]

Easton states that every political system faces stress; but because of the kind of system it is the members of the system have the opportunity to respond to stress in such a way as to try to assure the persistence of some kind of a system for making and executing binding decisions. Stress occurs "when

35. *Ibid.*, See, Diagram in p. 75.

36. *Ibid.*, p. 77.

37. *Loc. cit.*

there is a danger that the essential variables will be pushed beyond...their *critical range*".[38] (emphasis in original). For a responding, self-regulating system the ideas of the essential variables and critical range are, indeed of great importance. But these ideas are at the same time reminiscent of the idea of equilibrium which Easton himself shuns as impracticable on the ground that it requires a degree of quantification which is not possible to attain in political science, at least at its present stage of development. Easton seems to be unaware of the fact that the idea of the critical range also warrants quantification. After all unless we can measure the quantum of stress which may push the essential variables beyond their critical range, the concepts of essential variables and the critical range become redundant. Easton's concept of a political system with essential variables and a critical range is open to the same criticism which he himself offers against the equilibrium framework.

The concept of stress necessitates investigation of its source. Easton maintains that the sources of stress could be internal or external depending upon the position in which they originate. The conflicts over political instrumentalities are identified as internal stress and disturbance occuring as a result of influences from outside the system is called external stress.[39] Easton views disturbance as the cause of all stress. "Disturbances" according to Easton, "will refer to all activities in the environment or within a system that can be expected to or do displace a system from its current pattern of operations, regardless of whether or not it is stressful for the system."[40] Such disturbances could be neutral, benign, or stressful according to the degree to which they effect the chances for some or any kind of political system to persist.

Stressful disturbance is one which threatens to prevent a system from functioning. Stress for Easton is variation from

38. Easton, *A Systems Analysis of Political Life*, *op. cit.*, p. 24.
39. Easton, *Framework of Political Analysis*, *op. cit.*, pp. 80-82.
40. *Ibid.*, pp. 90-91.

the 'normal range of operation'.[41] As long as the 'essential variables' could be kept operating within the 'critical range' the system persists. The question which naturally arises is how are the sources of stress to be identified? In Easton's model they could be identified with the help of the concepts of 'inputs' and 'outputs'. These are the two linkage variables which link the political system and its environment. Here, the political system is being viewed as a flow model where happenings in the environment effects the political system through influences that flow into the system. These intakes are then converted into outputs through the structures and processes. Outputs are identified as authoritative decisions and their implementations. The outputs either return to the systems in the environment or turn back upon the system itself.[42]

With the help of the concept of inputs Easton hopes to delineate how behaviour in the various sectors of society affects what happens in the political sector. "Inputs", according to him, "will serve as summary variables that concentrate and reflect everything in the environment which is relevant to political stress".[43] He uses the concept of 'within puts' to delineate the disturbances occurring inside the system itself. Both the inputs and withinputs are sources of stress. The outputs influence events in the environment of the political system, and thereby help to determine each succeeding round of inputs into the system. There is, thus, a feedback loop in this model. The major inputs are demands and supports. He describes outputs as the decisions and actions of the authorities.

The disturbances created by stress are regulated by the political system through structural regulators, which he calls 'gate keepers' like interest groups, parties, opinion leaders or the mass media in the modern societies and notables, aristocr-

41. *Ibid*, p. 91.
42. *Ibid*., pp. 91-92.
43. *Ibid*., p. 111.

acy, or military cadre in traditional ones.[44] Cultural restraints and processes of combination of demands are also considered regulatory processes.[45] Here, in his bid to give his model a systemic character Easton seems to have over looked the fact that the agencies which combine demands, and as a result are expected to act as gatekeepers instead of regulating stress may at times contribute to intensification of stress on the system. Some purely pro-system gate-keepers, like cultural restraints, may be able to reduce pressure on the system; but in many cases the so-called gate-keepers may open flood gate of stress. He fails to note that gate-keepers like interest groups may reduce the number of demands but they do increase the intensity of demands by way of articulating them, and thereby increase stress on the system.

Not only an increase in demands but a fall in support may also lead to stress. It is, therefore, necessary for the system to regulate stress by way of sustaining support. Easton says that a regulative response with regard to support may include efforts to change the structures and processes that characterise a particular type of political system. A system may also regulate this kind of stress by building a diffuse support on the basis of sentiments of legitimacy, recognition of general welfare and a sense of political community. Finally, a system may use inputs to generate specific support and thereby regulate stress.[46]

Support is directed to the components or the basic political objects of the political system.[47] In a detailed discussion of these three components of the political system Easton takes up the political community first. This term "will refer to that aspect of a political system that consists of its members seen as a group of persons bound together by a political

44. *Ibid.*, p. 122.
45. *Ibid.*, p 123.
46. *Ibid.*, p. 125.
47. Easton, *A Systems Analysis of PoliticaLife*,..p^d *ol cit.*, 157.

division of labour".[48] A political system under investigation could be a small municipality, a nation state or an international political system. Each one of these systems will have a different range. As a component of the political system the range of the political community will vary according to the range of the system under study.[49]

A political community is distinguishable from a constitutional order. The constitutional order is now called a regime—another component of the political system. The members of any political system, "would need to accept some basic procedures and rules relating to the means through which controversy over demands was to be regulated and work out some ends that would at least broadly and generally guide the search for such settlements".[50] Regime is the order which encompasses these procedures and rules. Easton identifies three components of the regime; they are—values, which includes goals and principles; norms; and structures of authority. Easton says :

> The *values* serve as broad limits with regard to what can be taken for granted in the guidance of day to day policy without violating deep feelings of important segments of the community. The *norms* specify the kinds of procedures that are expected and acceptable in the processing and implementation of demands. The *structures of authority* designate the formal and informal patterns in which power is distributed and organized with regard to the authoritative making and implementing of decisions—the roles and other relationships through which authority is distributed and exercised[51] (emphasis added).

The third political object, authorities are the occupants of authority roles. Trying to be specific Easton says, "in practice,

48. *Ibid.*, p. 177.
49. *Ibid.*, p. 181.
50. *Ibid.*, p. 191.
51. *Ibid.*, p. 123.

we frequently identify them as the government of a country or group but there is need for a term with a broader scope than that implied in the concept of 'Government'[52] Easton distinguishes between the occupants of authority roles and the roles themselves—to qualify for inclusion in this term the occupants of authority roles must engage in daily affairs. They must be recognized by most members of the system as having responsibility for these matters and there actions must be accepted as binding most of the time by most of the members as long they act within the limits of their roles. Regulation of stress on these three components of the system enables the system to persist.

As a responding and self regulating system the political system is capable of absorbing change. So long as it is able to absorb change, it may be considered to have capacity for persistence. A system may undergo changes; but so long as it continues to authoritatively allocate values for a society it is considered as persisting. Easton maintains that change of a system, in his approach, will mean change of one or another of these objects and only where all objects change simultaneously the former system will be considered to have totally disappeared. Conversely a system may persist *'In Toto'* or only with respect to one of its basic objects.[53]

In other words—if a political system faces serious threat as a result of lack of support for the authorities the system may change the authorities while the regime and the political community may remain in tact. The same thing may happen in the case of lack of support for any of the other two components of the political system also. If the regime or the political community of a political system fails to muster enough support and if its feedback loop works properly, according to Easton's scheme of things the system should be able to modify its regime or the political community as the case may be. But are these components of the political system as pliable as Easton considers them to be ? As we have already noted that Easton himself explains that these components of the political system

52. *Ibid* , p. 212.
53. *Ibid.*, p. 172.

are political objects. What he seems to ignore is that as political objects they protect certain interests against others. Each one of these political objects are a part of an arrangement through which a particular political order is maintained. Authorities occupy a key role in the day to day affairs of this process. They take decisions and implement them. In this sense they are the most obvious aspect of this process. Exceptions apart, they have to operate within the rules of the game set by the regime. The regime as Easton rightly points out is composed of the values, norms and the structures of authority. These are decided upon, in some sense, by the political community. Easton's use of the term suggests that the community develops some kind of a consensus about these things. This question we intend to take up when we discuss the roles of consensus and conflict in Easton's model. To come back to the question of political community, Easton defines it as a political division of labour. It is "a plurality of relationships through which the individual members are linked to each other and through which the political objectives of the system are pursued".[54] Political objectives are of course instruments of material benefits ; but that again is a separate issue. For the fulfilment of these political objectives the political community establishes, what Easton calls, the regime and the regime operates through the authorities. The structure could be understood with the help of the following diagram.

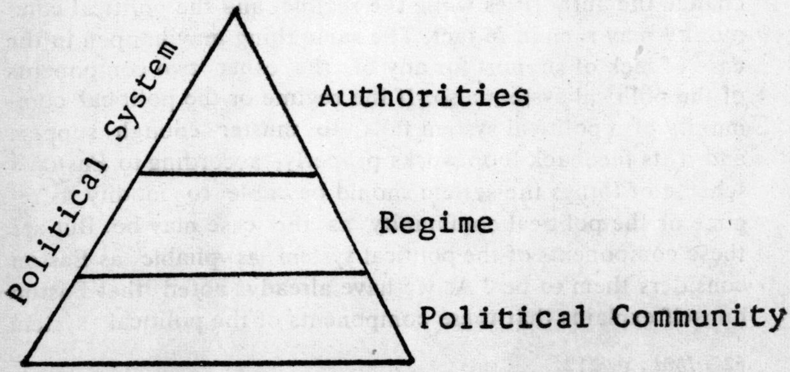

54. *Ibid.*, p. 177.

The political community is the basis of this structure. It is the foundation, the basis, on which the rest of the structure is built and hinges. Any change in the political community will therefore affect a total change in the system. In fact the system will disappear. The authorities may come and go. They are instruments of the implementation of the regime goals. If the occupants of the authority roles prove to be inefficient and if they do not apply the basic rules there will be discontentment among the members of the political community. As a result, the old authorities may be replaced by new ones. Such changes are frequent in modern times. It is possible that in a certain political system the regime and the authorities become identical for a period and in that case a change in the authorities may bring a change in the regime also. But much incidents are exceptions only. As a more important aspect of the political system the regime determines the long term goals of the system. Therefore, changes in regime are not as frequent. If the political community finds that the present regime cannot fulfil its goals any longer or that it can't protect the interests, protection of which is the basis of the community itself, it may decide to change the regime. A change of regime, in most cases, will force a change of the authorities. Because authorities, normally remain in their position only because they accept the regime.

However, such changes may not be as smooth as it appears to be. Since the regime protects vital interests any move to change a particular regime will be met with stiff opposition from those whose interests it protects. Sometimes even a change in the authorities may threaten to hurt so much of in:erest that it may even dismember a political community.

The most fundamental change that can take place in a political system is that of the political community. In comparison to this change the changes in the other two political objects are minor. In a sense Easton recognizes this. While discussing the use of the concept by K.W. Deutsch and E.B. Haas Easton maintains that these two authors used the term as some kind of a synonym of the political system. But his own use of the term is different from their use of it. He writes, "I wish to reserve 'Political Community' for the special purpose of identifying only one aspect of a political system, as one of a number of basic political objects towards which support may be extended or from which it may be withdrawn".[55] He then explains that to enable itself to muster support the system may effect necessary changes in each one of these political objects. It is interesting to note that while he gives us a detailed discussion of how authorities and regimes change to enable the system to persist[56] he does not do the same for political community. He merely shows how the political community attempts to build support for itself.[57] The only place where he discussed the possibility of a change in the political community to facilitate system persistence is one where he cites the example of the American Civil War as a change of the political community.[58] However, the example seem to be an unfortunate one. It is true that the defeat of the south in the civil war enhanced the process of change in the American Society. But the changes that brought rapid industrialization should not be confused with a change in the political community. Actually the prevailing 'political division of labour' even in the pre-civil war America was one that favoured industrialization. The political forces that came to dominate American politics ever since the adoption of the federal constitution were the forces that wanted development of industry and capitalism.[59] The

55. *Ibid.*, p. 57.
56. *Ibid.*, CF 179, 320.
57. *Ibid.*, pp. 325-340.
58. *Ibid.*, p. 179.
59. The tendencies of the political community to protect and foster the interest of the manufacturers were reflected in Hamilton's report on manufacturers in 1790. Hamilton's arguments could not clinch the issue at that time, but his ideas came to stay. Some of his policies as the Secretary of the Treasury set the ball rolling in favour industry and capital. For a discussion on this point See, S.E. Morrison and H.S. Commager, *The Growth of the American Republic* (Oxford University Press, New York, 1962), p. 327.Nye and Morpurgo also point out that "the American people have never accepted Government by aristocrates but they have

civil war was in fact the result of an attempt by the South to stall this trend. Therefore, if the farmers had won the war there would have been a major change in the American political community, or the political division of labour. In that case instead of protecting the interest of the manufacturers the political community in America would have come to promote the interests of the farmers. That would have changed the nature of the American political economy from one that wanted industrialization and associated changes to one that would favour an aggrarian economy and associated stagnancy. The Civil War, therefore, was an unsuccessful attempt to change the prevailing political community only.

Conflicts about the nature of political community or the political division of labour may lead to such strifes that the old political community may disappear in the sense that a new political division of labour may emerge. This, of course, will mean a change in the regime and the authorities also. In other words the character of the whole political system will change. In such a case it will be difficult to maintain that the system has persisted. In fact it is not possible to view a situation when the political community undergoes a change but the system persists.

Persistence is the central issue in Easton's analysis. He maintains that political science must understand the life processes of the political system as such. These processes are being identified as the defining functions of political system, the processes that assure "the perpetuation of any means through which values may be authoritatively allocated that is to permit the system to persist ?"[60]

Easton defines persistence, as often happens in political thought, with the help of its negative—non-persistence. He

maintained to this day the Hamiltonian faith in Government for Capitalists". R.B. Nye and J.E. Morpurgo, *A History of the United States, op. cit.*, Vol. 2, p. 260.

60. Easton, *A Framework of Political Analysis, op. cit*, p. 78.

hold that there is an advantage in doing so. He interprets the negative of persistence as the complete disappearance of a system.[61] Disappearance, here, means a total destruction. He uses examples of natural calamities to explain such a situation "it has occurred when the membership of a society has been utterly destroyed through some natural catastrophe such as an earthquake or epidemic, or when the society has failed to reproduce itself biologically, as perhaps in the case of Mesaverde Indians.[62]

In this discussion of "non-persistence" Easton seems to have missed the point that disappearance of a community during such natural calamities does not destroy the political community only ; it destroys the community as such. The disappearance of a political community must refer to a situation in which the political community disappears without the disappearance of the people inhabiting that area.

Though Easton has referred also to the Russian and the French revolutions, Germany at the end of the World War II and the Belgium Congo as cases of failure to persist ; his main examples as converse shows are those of natural catastrophe[63] converse rightly points out that Easton could not afford to use the term persistence to mean stability, maintenance of specific structures or equilibrium because that, he thought, may bring a status-quo bias. We shall, however, see in the next chapter that despite his conscious bid to avoid such a bias his model remains status-quoist in nature. Moreover, as Thorson shows, if we accept Easton's definition of persistence even a situation like the French revolution will have to be explained away as a change which enables the system to persist. To quote Thorson:

> There was an 'authoritative allocation of values' for France both in the time of Louis XVI and in the time of the First

61. *Ibid.*, p. 82.

62. *Ibid.*, *op. cit.*

63. Philip converse : *Book Review in American Political Review* (December 1965) Vol. LIX No. 4, pp. 1001-1002.

Republic, and we must conclude therefore that the 'very life Processes' of the French political system *persisted*—not, it must be said, because of anything that happened in France but because Easton's definition continues to apply.[64] (Emphasis in original).

If we accept Easton's definitions of the political system and his idea of persistence, a system will fail to persist only when the whole society disappears. Mackenzie also supports this view when he says "a break down of the political system involves a break down of the society".[65] Easton lands up in this difficult situation because his definitions of the life processes of political system, which enables the system to persist and politics are identical. Politics for him is the authoritative allocation of values. The life processes of political system are the "allocative processes and structures". These are the life processes of any or all systems.[66] Thorson makes the point succinctly when he says,

> ...Easton is obliged to say...that, in his sense of the term 'persist' a political system fails to persist when and when only his definition of politics fails to apply. But—and this is all important—this definition of politics is meant to be general, to apply to any case whatsoever. We are led therefore, to the following conclusions. The political system fails to persist when there is no longer any politics, or politics fails to persist, when there is no politics, or politics persists when it persists.[67]

It is only natural that such a framework will prove to be incapable of explaining anything worthwhile. Thorson shows that this framework is unable to explain basic changes that take place in the political life. According to Thorson Easton

64. Thorson, *op. cit.*, pp. 65-66.
65. W.J.M. Mackenzie, *Study of Political Science Today*, (London, 1970), p. 105.
66. Easton, *A Framework of Political Analysis*, *op. cit.*, p. 78.
67. Thorson, *op. cit.*, pp. 64-65.

is contemptuous of a theory of change. He says that Easton's theory merely supplied terminology capable of describing that such and such changes occurred but it can explain no political change whatsoever.[68] The futility of Easton's exercises becomes evident when Thorson quotes Easton himself to the effect that this approach to the analysis of political system does not help us to understand why any specific policies are adopted by the politically relevant members in a system.[69] If a framework of political analysis cannot explain any change, if it cannot help us to understand why particular policies are adopted, what purpose does it serve ? What theoretically relevant knowledge does it give us ? Nothing whatsoever. That is why Thorson calls Easton's enterprise futile.[70] Thorson attributes this to Easton's adoption of "the prediction generalization model of science."[71] According to Thorson the prediction generalization model of science is one which assumes that if a generalization is to qualify as a law, as a universal generalization, it must by definition be timeless in the sense that it applies at any time whatsoever.[72] Thorson maintains that Easton's idea of system is derived from biology. He further argues that the physiological system is a clear case of prediction generalization model.[73] If we accept Thorson's argument that the failure of Easton's model could be attributed to its prediction generalization roots then systems approach in physiology, would also have met the same fate. But in Thorson's own admission systems approach is physiology does serve some purpose.[74] It would, therefore, be wrong to conclude that the cause of the malady lies in the prediction generalization view of science.

68. *Ibid.*, p. 68.

69. *loc. cit.*

70. *Ibid*, pp. 70-71.

71. *loc cit.*

72. *Ibid.*, p. 51.

73. *Ibid.*, p. 59.

74. *loc. cit.*

The systems approach in Biology, from which Easton seems to have borrowed his model, is in fact, a branch of what is known as the general systems theory. Like the general system theory, systems thinking in Biology also aims at Unity of Sciences. Ludwig Von Bertalantfy a pioneer in this field emphasizes the integration of scientific knowledge. He spells out the main objectives of this approach in five propositions.

1. There is a general tendency towards integration in the various sciences, natural and social.

2. Such integration seems to be central in a general theory of systems.

3. Such theory may be an important means for aiming at exact theory in the non-physical fields of science.

4. Developing unifying principles running 'vertically' through the universe of the individual sciences, this theory brings us near to the goal of unity of sciences.

5. This can lead to a much needed integration of scientific education.[75]

Easton adopts the vocabulary of systems theory. But his approach does not follow the exact line of general systems theory. Evolution of Easton's ideas did produce some minor academic developments that are not fully identical with systems theory in its nature form. These developments include an extended flirtation with the movement known as behavioural science. Easton asserts that his is a behavioural science of politics ;[76] but the differences between his systems approach and that of the general systems theorists are of more serious nature with equally serious consequences.

75. Ludwig von Bertalanfly, *General Systems Theory, Foundations, Development, Applications*, (New York, 1968), p. 37.

76. Easton, *The Political System, op. cit.*, pp. 323-377 and "Systems Analysis in Politics and Its Critics", *op. cit.*, p. 25.

We have noted above that a major objective of the general systems theory has been the integration of Scientific knowledge. It will be unfair if we say that Easton is not aware of this tendency towards integration. In *A Framework of Political Analysis he* tried to explain that as an impact of the behavioural approach an integration of the social sciences was taking place at three different levels. At the applied level one could bring the data of social sciences together for the solution of whole social problems. At the level of research training students would be expected to address themselves not to a discipline but to social problems in the hope that they would learn to bear in mind the modes of analysis and data from any are of knowledge and research that seemed relevant and appropriate. At a third level training of a person in two or three disciplines might bring about a limited integration in the mind of a single individual.[77] Easton maintains that this trend led to a search for a unit of analysis that could be utilized in many of the disciplines. He refers to the use of actions, decisions and function as alternative units of analysis and then says,

> most recently, 'systems' have made their appearance as a focus, beginning with the smallest cell in the human body as a system and working up through even more inclusive systems such as the human being as an organism, the human personality, small groups, broader institutions, societies, and collection of societies such as the international systems.[78]

Easton explains this trend as an impact of the behavioural approach. But he fails to realize that the trend towards integration under the systems frame emanates from its holistic roots. Systems approach is closely related to holism ; because it attempts to explain the phenomenon under study in terms of a whole. There are three different types of holism. Holism I believes in five inter-related ideas.

77. Easton, *A Framework of Political Analysis*, *op. cit*, p. 14.
78. *Ibid.*, pp. 15-16.

1. The analytic approach as typified by the physico-chemical sciences proves inadequate when applied to certain cases for example, to biological organism, to society or even to reality as a whole.

2. The whole is more than the sum of its parts.

3. The whole determines the nature of its parts.

4. The parts cannot be understood if considered in isolation from the whole.

5. The parts are dynamically inter-related or inter-dependent.

Holism II believes that a whole, even after it is studied, cannot be explained in terms of its parts. Holism III holds that it is necessary to have terms referring to whole and their properties.[79]

The founders of general systems theory propagate ideas which adhere to one or the other of these three holistic positions. They have a holistic view of the reality. They use the concept 'system' to enable themselves to understand this reality. In other words they base their idea of the system on the empirical reality of the wholes. In this sense a systems approach is necessary to understand the phenomena under study.

Easton's approach is strikingly different from this position. He argues that if we look at the political life as a system it will be possible for us to isolate political phenomena for the purpose of study. We have already noted that he views political life as a system not because he believes that in reality it forms a system but because it is convenient to do so. This becomes evident also when he says "at first sight, to be sure, and, for that matter, even upon closer examination, Political

79. See, D.C. Phillips, *Holistic Thought in Social Science*, (New York, 1977), pp. 5-37.

Science does not seem to possess this systemic coherence".[80] He is aware of the fact that all social life is interdependent and it is artificial to isolate any set of social relations for specific attention. But he emphasizes that this artificiality is imposed upon political scientists by the need for a simplification of their data.[81] Easton uses the concept of system to serve this purpose. The difference with the general systems theory is, clear. The latter adopts 'system' as a part of a holistic approach which will ultimately lead to unification of scientific knowledge. Easton uses the concept to delimit the field of political science. He aims at isolating political phenomena for the purpose of study while general system theorists aims at its direct opposite.

Easton's model is meant to be analytical. It is not based on any determinate political system. It is an abstract theoretical construct. To put it in the words of Meehan, "Easton's Political System turns out to be an abstraction whose relation to empirical politics is virtually impossible to establish. The promise of a conceptual framework with 'high empirical relevance' simply has not been fulfilled".[82]

Thus by breaking away from the holistic tradition of the systems thinking Easton has developed a framework which is so general in nature that his whole exercise turns out to be a futile one. Easton could have saved himself from this situation only if he had focused on the determinate political systems. Because in that case he would not have tried to build an all time all place general theory of politics and as a result he would have developed an empirically relevant model. His effort at finding a general system makes his political science metaphysical. To quote Colletti :

> ...metaphysics never produces an effective analysis since for it, strictly speaking, facts no longer exist ; or, more

80. Easton, *The Political System, op. cit.*, p. 98.
81. *Ibid* , p. 97.
82. Meehan, *op. cit.*, pp. 173-74.

> precisely, because in the place of concrete historical phenomena it has interpolated the idea ; in the place of a concrete determinate society it has substituted society in general.[83]

Easton does precisely this. Instead of focusing on determinate political systems he focuses on the political system in general. In the place of the historical phenomena of the determinate political systems he has interpolated the idea of a political system in general and thereby he carries his theory to the realm of metaphysics. Had he focused on the determinate political systems his idea of political system would have been closer to reality. But such an approach would bring a status-quo bias to his analysis. Easton, in his works published in 1965 and later, has been making a conscious attempt to save himself from the possibility of being branded as a status-quoist. Ironically, despite all his attempts to rise above this bias his framework remains status quoist. This issue we propose to discuss in the next chapter.

83. Lucio Colletti, *From Rousseau to Lenin* (Delhi, 1969), p. 4.

CHAPTER 6

Status-Quo Bias : The Predicament of a Systems Analyst

In the preceding chapter we have seen that Easton chooses "Systems Analysis" as his approach to political theory. This choice brings a conservative bias to his political science. Ever since its emergence in the social sciences, systems paradigm has been criticized for its maintenance bias. Critics have pointed out that this model is incapable of explaining social confiict and more particularly the processes of fundamental social change. A related issue has been that it assumes the existence of an equilibrating mechanism in the systems under study.[1] These criticisms are invited by the very idea of "System". All systems do have boundaries. These boundaries separate them from their environments. The concept of system implies that it tends to maintain itself through various processes whenever it is disturbed, either from within or without its boundaries.

1. For these criticism See, J. Rex, *Key Problems in Sociological Theory*, (London, 1961) Chapters 6 & 7 ; J. C. Harsanyi, "Rational Choice Models of Political Behaviour Vs Functional and Conformist Theories" *World Politics*, Vol. 21 No. 4 (July 1969) pp. 513-538 ; Ralf Dahrendorf, *op. cit.*, pp. 107-128.

The question of maintenance, therefore, occupies an important position in all systems analysis. An analysis of Easton's approach would reveal that in his analysis there are two different approaches to the question of maintenance—one concerns itself with maintenance as such, the other aims at understanding how political systems manage to persist through change.

Concern for Maintenance

In an essay published in 1957[2] Easton makes his first attempt to develop a framework for the study of political systems. In this essay, he defines political life as a system of political actions. He holds that what enables the system to maintain itself are the inputs of various kinds to quote Easton :

> These inputs are converted by the process of the system into outputs and those, in turn, have consequences both for the system and for the environment in which the system exists. The formula here is very simple but as I hope to show also very illuminating. *Inputs-Political Systems or processes-outputs*.[3] (Emphasis added)

It is clear that in this formula the political system is viewed as the "Processes" that convert inputs into outputs. Easton's systems analysis aims at finding out how these processes maintain themselves. In other words his analysis seeks to find out how the system maintains itself. Easton sets this as one of the objectives of his analysis. While discussing inputs, Easton says that a political system must have continuing inputs to keep it going. He then writes :

> The specific research task in this connection would be to identify the inputs and the forces that shape and change them, *to trace the processes through which they are trans-*

2. Easton, "An Approach to the study of Political System", *op. cit.*

3. *Ibid.*, p. 6.

formed into out puts, to describe the general conditions under which such processes can be maintained, and to establish the relationship between outputs and succeeding inputs of the system.[4] (emphasis added).

If the political system comprises these processes and if Easton is interested in finding out "the general conditions under which such processes can be maintained", then he is interested in finding the general conditions under which the political system maintains itself. This does give a maintenance bias to his framework. It could, of course, be argued on Easton's behalf that his analysis aims at finding out only how these processes maintain themselves in general irrespective of the maintenance or non-maintenance of a particular political process. Therefore, it is possible for him to claim that his framework does not aim at inquiring into the conditions of maintenance of a particular process or system. But if we examine his comments about integration of political systems, it becomes crystal clear that his concern for the maintenance of these processes amounts to a concern for maintenance of determinate political systems. Easton is of the opinion that because of the structural differentiations present in political systems some amount of integration is necessary for each system. He hypothesizes, *if a structured system is to maintain itself*, it must provide mechanisms whereby its members are integrated or induced to co-operate in some minimal level so that they can make authoritative decisions".[5] (emphasis added).

The phrase 'structured system' can't refer to the processes in general. It can refer only to a particular process with its own structures. Therefore, structured system here would mean a determinate system only. These comments must, then, be read to mean that, political systems do provide mechanisms through which such integration help the systems

4. *Ibid.*, p. 8.

5. *Ibid.*, p. 9.

to maintain themselves. Such an approach can't view the political system as one that can undergo changes.

In this essay Easton's discussion of support as a kind of inputs also reflects his concern for system maintenance. He identifies two kinds of basic inputs of political systems. They are demands and supports.[6] In the preceding chapter we have discussed these inputs and their role in Easton's framework. Here the only point that concerns us is Easton's views about support as a mechanism of system maintenance. For him support constitutes either of overt actions or orientations or states of mind. This supportive state of mind is a deep seated set of attitudes or pre-dispositions which helps the system to maintain itself. He writes, "supportive states of mind are vital inputs for the *operation and maintenance of a political system*"[7] (emphasis added). Easton then goes on to assert that it is necessary to identify that typical mechanisms through which supportive attitudes are inculcated and continuously reinforced within a political system.[8] Identification of such mechanisms would, of course, help the system to maintain itself.

We have already noted that in Easton's framework the political system converts inputs into outputs. These outputs act as inducement for supportive attitudes. To quote Easton, "outputs consisting of political decisions, constitute a body of specific inducements for the members of a system to support that system".[9] But he is also aware that the level of support is not always dependent exclusively upon the outputs. If we assume that the outputs are the sole determinants of the level of support then, as Easton says, "we could scarcely account for the maintenance of the numerous political systems in which satisfaction of demands has been manifestly low, in which

6. *Loc. cit.*

7. *Ibid.*, p. 12.

8. *Loc. cit.*

9. *Ibid.*, p. 15.

public coercion is limited and yet which have endured for epochs".[10] Here again Easton's concern for the maintenance of political systems is evident; but what is more important is that he is suggesting the existence of some other means besides outputs through which systems build up mechanisms for self-maintenance.

Easton suggests that even when the political systems fail to produce outputs which can maintain the necessary level of supports they may be able to maintain themselves through, what he calls, 'politicization' or socialization. This term is defined as the process through which members of the society learn political patterns. He says, "through it a person learns to play his political roles which include the absorption of the proper political attitudes".[11] These political attitudes on the other hand are viewed as generating and accumulating a strong reserve of support. He perceives politicization as the process through which attachments to a political system becomes built in to the maturing members of a society. He suggests that these attachments enable the system to acquire legitimacy. A system, Easton believes, is accepted as legitimate only when the basic political attachments become deeply rooted or institutionalized. Legitimacy contributes to the maintenance of the system. The following quotation makes the point clear :

> ...it is an empirical observation that in those instances where political systems have survived the longest support has been mobilised by an organised belief in the legitimacy of the relevant government and regimes.[12]

Though this is an empirical observation and not a normative concern for maintenance, this observation becomes relevant to his framework only in the context of his overall concern for maintenance. If the focus is on "legitimacy of

10. *Ibid.*, p. 16.
11. *Ibid.*, p. 17.
12. *Ibid.*, p. 18.

the relevant governments and regimes" then the concern is definitely for determinate political systems. When a system builds up legitimacy for a particular government or a particular regime it actually builds up legitimacy for that particular system. It is implied in Easton's argument that lack of legitimacy for government and regime would mean lack of legitimacy for the system itself. If legitimacy helps in maintenance of systems; it helps determinate systems only.

Easton suggests that it is necessary to understand the role of legitimacy for an understanding of the political life and the answer to questions concerning the formation, maintenance, transmission and change of the standard of legitimacy will contribute generally to "an understanding of the way in which support is sufficiently institutionalized so that a system may regularly and without excessive expenditure of effort, transform inputs of demands into outputs of decisions".[13] Since this conversion process is the political system itself, by studying legitimacy in this manner we shall be able to understand how systems manage to maintain themselves.

The crucial question that he asks about the support to systems also indicates that he is interested in finding out how systems maintains themselves. Easton holds that support is necessary for system maintenance. He asks "how do systems typically manage to maintain a steady flow of support?" He then comments that without support a system will not absorb sufficient energy from its members to be able to convert demands into decisions.[14] If support enables the systems to maintain themselves and if Easton's analysis aims at finding out how a steady flow of support is maintained then his analysis is concerned with the maintenance of political systems. An enquiry into how political systems maintain themselves may not have any normative bias. It could be argued that such an inquiry may in fact help in finding out how to change them. But such a concern with maintenance in a framework

13. *Ibid.*, p. 18.
14. *Ibid.*, p. 15.

assumes that if the inputs keep on coming and right outputs are produced a system will continue to maintain itself. Maintenance then is viewed as the normal state; change is viewed as an aberration only. As Allen says, "The conceptual approach which assumes reality as basically static provides the framework for theoretical explanations which explains and justify the status-quo."[15]

Role of Consensus :

We have seen that Easton defines support as *a state of mind*. He also believes that politicization leads to absorption of proper political attitudes. These ideas bring an element of consensus to his framework. A state of mind could not be imposed nor can absorption of proper political attitudes effected by force. Unless members of a system accept a particular set of values creation of a particular state of mind or absorption of proper attitudes are not possible. From this point of view a political system needs to be positively accepted by members.

Easton's treatment of the three objects of support makes this point further clear. According to Easton, support is fed into the political system in relation to three objects—the community, the regime, and the government. We have discussed these in the preceding chapter. Here we are concerned only with the role that consensus plays in the functioning of these objects.

In his discussion of these objects Easton takes up the political community first. He says, "no political system can continue to operate unless its members are *willing to support the existence of a group* that seeks to settle differences or promote decisions through peaceful action in common".[15a] (emphasis added). This phenomenon is referred to as the

15. Allen, *op. cit.*, p. 44.

15a. Easton, "*An Approach to the Study of Political Systems*" *op cit.*, p. 12.

political community. If it is assumed that the members of the political systems need to support such a group willingly, then it follows that there must be some consensus about it. Easton speaks of the willingness of the people, and willingness cannot be created by force.

The second object of support, Regime, is also viewed as based on a consensus. A regime in the Eastonian sense is consisted of all those arrangements that regulate the way in which demands put into the system are settled and the way in which decisions are put into effect. These arrangements are often called the rules of the game. It is in the light of these rules that actions by members of the system are legitimated and accepted by the bulk of the members as authoritative. "Unless there is a minimum convergence of attitudes in support of these fundamental rules, the constitutional principles, as we call them in Western society, there would be insufficient *harmony in the actions of the members* of a system to meet the problems generated by their support of a political community".[16] (Emphasis added), such convergence of attitudes and harmony of actions among the members is possible only if there is a consensus. Easton admits this in the very next paragraph where he deals with the third object of support. The third object of support is the government.

> "If a political system is going to be able to handle the conflicting demands put into it, not only must the members of the system be prepared to support the settlement of these conflicts in common and *possess some consensus with regards to the rules governing the mode of settlement*; they must also be ready to support a government as it undertakes the concrete tasks involved in negotiating the settlements".[17] (emphasis added).

These rules governing the mode of settlement are the components of the regime. The consensus about these rules

16. *Ibid.*, p. 13.

17. *Ibid.*, p. 13.

then refers to a consensus about the regime. However, Easton does not suggest that governments rule only by consensus. They may elicit support in many ways. They may persuade, acquire consent, or manipulate support. "But", he says, "it is a familiar axiom of political science that government based upon force alone is not long for this world; it must buttress its position by inducing a favourable state of mind in its subjects through fair or foul means".[18] As we have argued above a state of mind cannot be imposed; it has to evolve. An approach that assumes that a government can continue for any length of time only if it can create such a state of mind implies that all continuing governments are run by and large on the basis of some consensus.

It is thus clear that in Easton's view supports for the political community, the regime, and the government in any lasting political system are based on some consensus about these three objects of support. He further, argues that support for these three objects are not independent of each other. They are closely intertwined. He is of the opinion that the presence of one is a function of the presence of one or both of the other types. In this sense they are indivisible. If supports for these three objects are intertwined and they are based on a consensus about each one of them, then it logically follows that the survival of the political system is also based on a consensus.

Role of Equilibrium :

Like consensus equilibrium too plays an important role in Eastons 1957 framework. It assumes that there is an equilibrating mechanism in every political system Easton is aware that the members of the political systems may be engaged in both supportive and hostile behaviour; but he is interested in finding out the net balance of support.[19] He also affirms that the input and the output balance is a vital mecha-

18. *Loc. cit.*

19. *Ibid.*, pp. 14-15.

nism in the life of a political system.[20] If the life of the system is dependent on such a balance it would imply that equilibrium plays an important role in the political system.

Moreover, Easton views the political system as an open system and such systems as, we shall see, entails the idea of equilibrium. He says, "to distinguish a political system from other social systems, we must be able to identify it by describing its fundamental units and establishing the boundaries that demarcate it from units outside the system".[21] It is not only that he sees the necessity of identifying these boundaries but he also considers the system as open to the influences from outside the boundary. He maintains, "the way in which a system works will be in part a function of its response to the total social, biological and physical environment".[22] If the system is one which responds to the influence of the environment it must be an open system. Ken Menzies says, 'an open system is boundary maintaining'.[23] An open and boundary maintaining system will necessarily have processes which will result in some features that serve to separate the system from its environment. Such features are the equilibria of the system.[24] Since Easton views the political systems as an open system, equilibrium necessarily plays an important role in his framework. The processes which enables the political system to make authoritative decisions, put together, are the features that serve to separate the system from its environment. This also is the point of equilibrium. So long as this equilibrium exists the authoritative decisions are possible. The decisions and the processes related to them are the features that separate the political system from its environment.

20. *Ibid*, p. 16.

21. *Ibid.*, p. 7.

22. *Loc. cit.*

23. Ken Menzies, *Talcott Parsons and Social Image of Man*, (London, 1976), p. 124.

24. *Ibid.*, p. 125.

Handerson defines equilibrium as "a state such that if a small modification different from that which will otherwise occur is impressed upon a system, a reaction will at once appear, tending towards conditions that would have existed if the modification had not been impressed".[25] Nagel also defines equilibrium point in similar terms.[26] If an equilibrium exists there will also be forces that tend to recreate the equilibrium if it is disturbed. This idea is clearly evident in Somerhoffs treatment of the "directive correlation". He explains directive correlation in terms of a system's capacity to respond to a range of possible variations in the environment so that the system attains a focal condition.[27]

Easton's political system as we have noted above is also viewed as a responsive system. It is capable of responding to a range of variations in the environment. Easton says, "much of what happen within a system has its birth in the efforts of the members of the system to cope with the changing environment".[28] Here Easton uses the analogy of the biological system to explain his point :

> In part, of course, the way in which the body works represents responses to needs that are generated by the very organization of its anatomy and functions; but in larger part, in order to understand both the structure and the working of the body, we must also be very sensitive to the inputs from the environments.[29]

25. Barber Bernard, (ed.), *L.J. Handerson on the Social System : Selected Writings* (Chicago, 1970), p. 28.
26. E.A. Nagel, "Formalization of functionalism with special reference to its Application in the Social Sciences", in N. Demareth and R. Peterson, (eds.) *System Change and Conflict : A Reader in Contemporary Sociological Theories, and the Debate Over Functionalism* (New York, 1957), pp. 47-53.
27. See, G. Sommerhoff, *Analytic Biology* (London, 1950).
28. Easton, "*An Approach to the Study of Political System*" *op. cit.*, p. 8.
29. *Ibid.*, p. 8.

In the biological system the concept of homeostasis plays an important role. It is assumed that there are a variety of mechanism to maintain fixed levels of blood-sugar, blood protein, fat and calcium as well as adequate supplies of oxygen, a constant body temperature. As Canon shows these mechanisms produce and restore homeostasis.[30] Easton's view endows this tendency to the political system. All mechanism of support and integration in fact are supposed to produce this kind of a homeostasis, a steady state or an equilibrium.

The Shift :

It is clear from the above discussion that the concern for inquiry into the conditions of system maintenance, the role of consensus in his treatment of the objects of support and support in general, and the idea of a boundary maintaining open system which brings in the notion of equilibrium or homeostasis give a maintenance bias to Easton's 1957 model for systems analysis His approach, however, underwent a change during the eight intervening years after which, in 1965, he published two major books.[31]

In these two books he emphasizes that his framework is not concerned with the system "Maintenance". He repeatedly asserts that systems analysis concerns itself with the question of system persistence and not system maintenance. He states in clear terms that there is a distinction between system *persistence* and system *maintenance*. He writes, "It is one matter to inquire into the conditions through which a system is able to maintain itself and quite another to seek to reveal the conditions of persistence".[32]

We have noted that in his 1957 essay he considers inquiry into the conditions of maintenance of political systems to be

30. W.B. Canon, *The Wisdom of the Body* (New York, 1963).
31. Easton, *A Framework of Political Analysis*, *op. cit. A Systems Analysis of Political Life*, *op. cit.*
32. Easton, *A Framework of Political Analysis*, *op. cit.*, p. 88.

the main task of research. In 1965 he sets a different objective for systems analysis. The central question he is concerned with now, is—"regardless of time or place, what makes it possible for a system to assure the perpetuation of any means through which values may be authoritatively allocated, that is to permit the system to persist?"[33] In 1957 he was concerned with maintenance of the structured system; but in 1965 he does not consider particular structures and patterns any more important. Now he considers the life processes of political system more important. He holds that the important question that must be inquired into is how these processes manage to persist.[34] Persistence is considered to be a much broader concept than maintenance : "The idea of persistence extends far beyond that of systems maintenance; it is oriented towards exploring change as well as stability both of which may be interpreted as alternative avenues for coping with stress".[35] Persistence thus allows for the possibility of the continuance of a system through change, whereas the concept of maintenance is devoid of any such possibility.

This point is further stressed by Easton in his :

A Systems Analysis of Political Life :

> "The perspectives of a systems analysis of political life impels us to address ourselves to the following kind of questions : How can any political system ever persist whether the world be one of stability or of change".[36]

The shift in his position regarding the main task of systems analysis is thus clear. He, of course, does not say it in so many words that his approach has undergone a change. However, the relevant question that arises is—why has Easton

33. *Ibid.*, p. 78.

34. *Ibid.*, p 88.

35. *Loc. cit.*

36. Easton, *A Systems Analyized Political Life, op. cit.*, pp, 14-15.

found it necessary to change his position? If systems analysis aims at enquiring into the conditions of maintenance of political systems then that will give it a static bias. Such a framework will fail to deal with change. Enquiry into the process of persistence opens up the possibility of accommodating change. Theoretically it is this necessity of accommodating the idea of change which makes Easton opt for persistence and shun maintenance.

To understand how Easton came to realize this problem we must look at what was happening in a sister discipline during the late the 1950's. Systems approach was introduced in sociology much before its emergence in political science. The term system had been used by Spencer himself. It occupied a central position in Pareto's sociology [37] Pitrim A. Sorokin also advocated the idea of a systemic sociology.[38] But it was Talcott Parsons who placed system in a seat of honour. He published his famous book, *The Social System*[39] in 1951. This book was an attempt at developing a systems theory of society. But before, 'system' could establish itself firmly in the discipline it came under fire. A number of critics pointed out its conservative bias.[40] It has been argued that systems theory in sociology aimed at providing a justification for the status-quo. They argued that it was obsessed

37. Nicholas S. Timasheff, *Sociological Theory* (New York, 1965), pp 230-263.

38. See, Pitrim A. Sorokin, *Contemporary Sociological Theories* (New York, 1928) and *Society Culture and Personality*, (Harper, New York, 1947).

39. Talcott Parsons, *The Social System* (New York, 1951).

40. See, David Lockwood, "Some Reflections on the Social System" *British Journal of Sociology*, Vol. VI (June 1956), pp. 134-146;

Ralf Dohrendorf "Out of Utopia : Toward A Reorientation of Sociological Analysis". *American Journal of Sociology* Vol. LXIV (1958), pp. 115-127.

Barrington Moore, *Political Power and Social Theory* (Cambridge Mass. 1958).

C.W. Mills, *The Sociological Imagination* (London, 1959).

with the idea of maintenance and failed to deal with change, that emphasis on consensus and equilibrium gave it a static bias. During the fifties most of these criticisms came from the European scholars and only with the publication of Barrington Moore and C. Wright Mills' books in the late fifties that the American sociology itself was enjoined.[41]

Easton's first model appeared in 1957 and the critiques of systems analysis in sociology by Moore and Mills appeared in 1958 and 1959 respectively. Though Easton does not refer to any of these critics of systems analysis in sociology and seems to be blissfully unaware of these developments his new approach must be understood in this background only. Easton's framework itself was not directly attacked; but Easton's incisive mind must have seen implicit in this on Parsons attack, a criticism of his framework too. This may have been the reason why in the later books he takes pains to distinguish between maintenance and persistence. Philip Converse while, reviewing Easton's *A Framework of Political Analysis* says that by opting for a broad concept of persistence Easton has successfully out flanked the critics of systems theory.[42] Converse, however, does not point out that Easton's approach has undergone a change.

In 1965, Easton consciously attempts to save his framework from the stigma of stability bias. He tries to do this by replacing the term maintenance with persistence. He writes that Maintenance is "too heavily charged" with the idea of stability and, quite alien to the idea of change. That is why he opts for a theory that "explains the capacities of a system to persist, not to maintain itself as this would be normally understood. It seeks a theory of persistence, not of self maintenance or equilibrium".[43]

41. See, Robert W. Friedrich, *A Sociology of Sociology* (New York, 1970), p. 26.

42. Philip, Converse, *op. cit.*

43. Easton, *A Framework of Political Analysis, op. cit.* p. 88.

This statement does not leave any scope for doubt that he is trying to respond to the line of criticism mentioned above. This, indeed, is an attempt to save his framework from a static bias. Whether he succeeds in doing so is a question which needs some discussion. We shall turn to that question presently.

Persistence of Status-quo bias :

In the books published in 1965, Easton displays an awareness of the fact that there is a danger of systems analysis becoming status-quoist. He attempts to avoid such a bias by focusing on the question of persistence instead of maintenance. But a mere change in terminology cannot transform an essentially static analysis into a dynamic one. That is way even in the 1965 volumes his framework remains static. Attempts at accommodating change by broadening the concept of persistence results merely, as we have noted in the preceding chapter, in swallowing all changes by 'system persistence'.

The question of system persistence, in the Eastonian sense, is the question of persistence of the life processes of systems. He writes, "Systems analysis is designed to clarify the consequences pertaining to the continued survival of some form of political life".[44] This of course implies that this kind of analysis is not concerned with the maintenance of determinate political systems and in that sense is not static in character. But despite this assertion this framework betrays a concern for maintenance of the systems under study. Moreover, the roles of consensus and equilibrium remains almost the same in this model also.

As in 1957 in 1965 also Easton views the political system as an open and responding system. He claims that the peculiar characteristic that political systems share with other social systems, and even some mechanical and biological ones, is

44. *Ibid.*, p. 89. In an interview with the present author Easton reiterates this position. See, Appendix.

that they are not necessarily defenseless in the face of disturbances to which they may be subjected.[45] Easton proposes to begin "by viewing political life as a system of behaviour imbedded in an environment to the influences of which the political system itself is exposed and in turn reacts".[46] Therefore, there is no scope for doubt about Easton's idea of a political system. It is an open boundary maintaining system, with a capacity to respond to stress.

As we have seen in our discussion of his 1957 model an approach that views the system as an open and responsive system can't do without the idea of equilibrium. Easton's treatment of support as an input also reveals that there is an element of homeostasis in his model. Support is considered a major index of stress; a fall in support would mean an increase in stress. "Where such support threatens to fall below a minimal level, regardless of the causes the system might either provide mechanism to revive flagging support or its days will be numbered."[47] This is in tune with his view of the political system as a responding and persisting system. If a political system needs such a mechanism to survive, all surviving systems must possess such a mechanism. This argument implies that if there is a fall in support there will be a tendency in the system to find alternative sources of support. The level of support which enables the system to persist is the point of equilibrium.

The equilibrium perspective is reflected in the idea of the "critical range" also. The allocation of values for a society and the relative frequency of compliance with them are the essential variables of political life. "Stress will be said to occur when there is a danger that the essential variables will be pushed beyond what we may designate as their *Critical range*".[48] (emphasis in original). If a system is to persist

45. *Ibid.*, p. 77.
46. Easton, *A Systems Analysis of Political Life*, *op. cit.*, pp. 17-18.
47. Easton, *A Framework of Political Analysis*, *op. cit.*, p. 124.
48. Easton, *A Systems Analysis of Political Life*, *op. cit.*, p. 24.

than it must keep these variables within this critical range. Easton's responding political system will take steps to maintain this situation. The system may try to do this by mobilizing support for the objects of support, regulating demands, politicizing members or making changes in one or more of the objects of support. Such changes are aimed at enabling the system to persist "...every persisting system has *homeostasis* devices to help it cope with stress".[49] (emphasis added)

Bottomore's statement about systems theory in sociology that "the essential idea upon which it rests is that every society should be conceived as a system in equilibrium; and that any disturbance of this equilibrium, if it occurs at all, should be seen as providing a responsive adaptation, so that equilibrium is restored and the society maintained in the original, or a slightly modified form",[50] is true of Easton's systems analysis also. He views the political system as such a responsive system based on an equilibrium.

An approach that views the political system in this manner tends to underplay the role of conflict in society. It emphasizes the role of group and cultural factors. Very often social order is explained in terms of group or interest satisfaction. As Barrington Moore puts it, "in equilibrium theory the key assumption is that any social system tends towards a state of rest in which the conflicts and strains among its component parts are reduced to a minimum".[51]

Continuance of any political system, in Easton's opinion, depends upon the flow of required support. We have noted in the preceding chapter that such support is oriented towards the three political objects. Easton's treatment of these objects shows that even in his 1965 works consensus plays a major role in his framework. He seems to believe that these objects

49. Easton, *A Framework of Political Analysis*, *op. cit.*, p. 95.
50. T.B. Bottomore, *Sociology and Social Criticism*, (New York, 1974), p. 20.
51. Moore, *Political Power and Social Theory*, *op. cit.*, p. 137.

and their smooth functioning is dependent on a consensus about their nature. The role of conflict and coercion is thus shown as almost non-existent. Support to these objects, in this view, is not extracted from the members. Easton suggests that members of political systems support these objects because they feel that they should support them. "The total input of support for a particular object is a *measure of the intensity of individual feelings* and behaviour together with the number of individuals involved..."[52] Easton, of course, does not imply that active support of all the members, or at least of a majority, is always necessary for persistence of a system. He is aware that a system may persist even with a minority support, provided there is no strong active opposition.[53] But such an approach plays down the role of coercion in political system. This approach gives the impression that all existing political systems are there because they are by and large accepted on the basis of some consensus. It seems to ignore the fact that very often coercion plays a dominant role in making a large section acquiesce, in the sense that they grudgingly agree to the prevailing arrangement.

In an attempt to define political community as an object of support Easton writes :

> In the first place, it contains the suggestion that a group of persons are for one reason or another joined together in a *common political enterprise*. If this were not implicit, there would be little reason for turning to the idea of a political community at all. *Community suggests co-operation of some sort*. In the second place, it also implies that the way in which the common enterprise is conducted may vary with respect to the degree of *cohesion or sense of community* the members feel. A community is usually something more than just an aggregate. It is a group that may be bound by the subtleties of sentiment.[54] (emphasis added).

52. Easton, *A Systems Analysis of Political Life, op. cit.*, p. 165.
53. *Ibid*, p. 166.
54. *Ibid.*, p. 177.

Here, the first implied notion, that is the common political enterprise is called by Easton "The Political community". The second, he calls "the sense of community". While the first needs only "cooperation of some sort", the second needs "cohesion". He views the sense of community only as a possible characteristic not an essential one. This would imply that what is necessary for the persistence of political system is cooperation of some sort, not cohesion or sense of community. This would make it appear as if Easton does not stress the need for consensus. "Cooperation of some sort" is possible even without a consensus; but "cohesion" and sense of community can develop only on the basis of a consensus. However, we need only to move a few pages ahead to find Easton emphasizing the importance of "sense of community". He says, "But if a sense of community fails to emerge and deepen over time, as a source of support, it may leave a system extremely vulnerable to stress".[55] He cites the case of the Austro-Hungarian empire as an example where coercion and material reward kept the system going; but in the long run, the input of support was insufficient to hold the community together as an unified political system when it came under stress of military defeat.[56]

The implication clearly is that if a system is to persist for any length of time, there must be a sense of community among its members. This is only one step short of saying that all persisting systems do have a sense of community. A sense of community, of course cannot be the result of unresolvable conflicts. The community cannot be coerced to develop such a sense. A feeling of solidarity resulting in political cooperation is possible only if the community has some consensus about the political division of labour. This mode of analysis creates the impression that a consensus regarding ends and means is the basis of a political community.

55. *Ibid.*, p. 187.

56. *Loc, cit.*

Easton's discussion of the second object of support also reveals the consensual element, Regime, as we have noted above in these pages, consisted of the rules of the game. Easton argues that every regime consists, in part, of a broadly defined underlying set of political values and principles, articulated or implicit, which impose constraints on the purpose for which the energies and the responses of the system may be committed. He asks "could a system persist without *some minimal agreement or at least acquiescence*, among the politically relevant members about the broad values within the context of which outputs would be acceptable?"[57] Though Easton uses the words "some minimal agreement or at least acquiescence", this must not lead us to believe that he views even acquiescence to the regime as sufficient for persistence of political systems. He goes on to explain that we cannot expect to find an universal agreement about values and goals. He says,

> It seems reasonable to assume *that systems will vary with respect to the degree of value consensus* they display and level of generality at which it appears and that the group whose values do, dominate, will also vary from a minority to a much larger number[58] (emphasis added),

If Easton holds that systems may vary with respect to value consensus then he is obviously implying that some consensus is necessary. He only points out the possibility of variety of value consensus. In another passage he says :

> In general, the very nomenclature used to classify systems democratic, communist, authoritarian, traditional and transitional, modernizing, autocratic and the like—high lights differnces in value premise of such systems.[59]

Value premises of various types of systems may vary but the thrust of the argument remains that in each determinate

57. *Ibid.*, p. 195.
58. *Ibid.*, p. 198.
59. *Ibid.*, p. 195.

political system there must be some value consensus on which the regime is based.

The third object of political support was called the government in 1957. Now, he calls it the authorities :

> Every system, we know, must be prepared to support some members who will be ready, willing, and able to pay some degree of special attention to seeing to it that differences are settled or handled in some way that is acceptable to the politically relevant at least [60]

The members of a system must provide enough support for these authorities; otherwise the system will fail to persist. But if the differences are settled in some way "that is acceptable to the politically relevant at least", then in all societies a large number of people who are politically not relevant will not willingly support the system. The system will have to resort to coercion to extract support from this section. Easton, however refuses to see this implication of his own argument. He argues that if the authorities impose themselves on the members it might work for a while but in the long run the support for the authorities must be based on the confidence of the members :

> If the members lose their *confidenee* in the ability of any authorities at all to cope with the problems of the day, the effect on support to other levels of the system may be serious at least for the persistence of that kind of system.[61] (emphasis added).

Confidence is a state of mind. It refers to a firm trust or belief. Such a trust or belief cannot be developed under coercion. It must come from within. Only if thers is some consensus about the authorities and their mode of operation among the members of a system, will they have such a confidence.

60. Ibid., p. 216.
61. *loc. cit.*

Easton's analysis of the mechanism of support towards these three objects of support and the attitude of members towards them reveals the important role that consensus plays in his model. This role of consensus has far reaching consequences for his framework. A social reality may be viewed as one perceived by consensus or one ridden with contradictions as Allen says :

> There is a qualitative difference between perceiving reality as consisting of systems pervaded by consensus with given structures capable of experiencing only limited changes in their superstructure, on the one hand and perceiving it as an interrelating entity, beset with contradictions which are capable of transforming it.[62]

A system which is based on consensus can neither have contradiction which could lead to qualitative changes nor can it allow possibility of confronting uncontrollable pressures for such changes from outside sources. To quote Allen again "such systems belong to the fantasy world of those who would like to put present structure in cotton wool and preserve them for ever".[63] This is not to suggest that there is no shared belief; there are. But they comprise a totality which possesses its own contradictions. There are attempts by social scientists at building, what is very often called, a conflict model of society as opposed to the consensus model.[64] But these attempts define and analyse conflict in a manner as to prevent social scientists from viewing conflict as capable of altering structures. They do not view conflict as a permanent feature of the social reality.[65] Why social reality must be viewed as beset with contradictions and how such a view is capable of

62. Allen, *Social Analysis*, *op. cit.*, p. 42.

63. *Ibid* , p. 40.

64. See, Lewis Coser, *The Functions of Social Conflict* (London, 1956) and Ralf Dahrendorf, *Class and Class Conflict in Industrial Society* (London, 1957).

65. Allen, *Social Analysis*, op. cit., pp. 43-50.

perceiving social reality as a changing phenomenon is an entirely different question and is beyond the scope of this work. The point here is that a consensus view of the society has a static bias in the sense that it assumes that there is a consensus about the prevailing structures and therefore a qualitative change is not only imminent, but is unnecessary. The consensual framework stresses a common obeisance by the general populace to values crucial to the society, acceptance of the basic legitimacy of existing structural forms, and suggests—while recognizing some differences and conflicts within society—the compatibility and reconciliability of differences rather than the possibility of non-compatible non-resolvable difference.[66] We can, therefore, conclude that despite his efforts to accommodate change and to remove the static bias from his framework by replacing the concept of system maintenance by system persistence, Easton's framework remains static. That is the predicament of a systems analyst—however much he may try to accommodate change his framework in the ultimate analysis remains status-quoist.

66. Malebsky Sandor, *Mass Society and Political Conflict*, (London, 1976), p. 235.

CHAPTER 7

Study of Political Socialization : Questionable Assumptions and Doubtful Conclusions

In the preceding chapters we have noted that Easton's search for reliable political knowledge has led him to an area of political theory which he calls systems analysis. He repeatedly states that the central question that concerns this analysis is how Political Systems manage to persist in a world of stability or of change ? He maintains that unless political systems can muster support for their authorities, regimes and political communities, they cannot persist. The question of persistence is thus related closely to the question of support for these political objects. Easton views the political system as capable of taking necessary steps to build up such support. In his writings on political socialization he systematically examines the processes through which such support is built.

As early as 1957, in his first attempt to develop a framework for political analysis, he argues that politicization is a "mechanism of support". He says :

It is essential for the validity of an orderly political system that the members of the system have some common basic expectations with regard to the standard that have to be used in making political evaluations to the way people will feel about various political matters, and to the way members of the system will perceive and interpret political phenomena. The mechanism through which this learning takes place is of considerable significance in understanding how a political system generates and accumulates strong reserve cf support.[1]

By politicization he means political socialization only. The point becomes clear when he says :

If we use the concept socialization to describe the process through which the individual passes as he becomes a full-fledged member of a society, we can identify that aspect of the process particularly relevant to the acquisition of roles as *political socialization or politicization*[2] (emphasis added).

Here Easton seems to have used the trems 'politicization' and 'political socialization' interchangeably. But these two terms do not mean the same thing. It will become clear during the course of our discussion that Easton himself does not always use these two terms inter-changeably. He uses the term 'politicization' to refer to the process through which the child becomes aware of the political authorities and begins to distinguish them from other authorities. He refers to political socialization as a means available to the political system for building up necessary support.

The idea of political socialization, thus occupies an important place in Easton's political science. He has written a large number of articles jointly with Robert Hess and Jack Dennis. These articles aim at empirical investigations and theoretical formulations. The investigations conducted with Jack Dennis

1. David Easton, "An Approach to the Analysis of Political System", *op. cit.*, p. 17.
2. David Easton, "The Function of Formal Education in a Political System", *The School Review* (Autumn 1957), p. 310.

are incorporated in a book.[3] While stating the purpose of this book the authors argue that if a political system is to persist it must be able to muster diffuse support. They then go on to say, "Our central purpose will be to investigate how this support is marshalled through the early socialization of those new to the system by virtue of their birth in it".[4] It is, therefore, clear that Easton views political socialization as a process through which the political system can build support vital for its own persistence.

The most important finding of the Easton and Dennis study is that in the American political system the children learn to support the structures of authorities. "Our data suggest that in the Uinted States a positively supportive image of the general structures of authority, is being widely and regularly reproduced for young new members"[5]. The American child, according to them, begins as a 'political primitive' with a vision of government as the embodiment of a man or a small set of men who constitute a dimly recognized form of external authority. While he grows he becomes familiar with popular institutions. He begins to learn what is outside and what is inside the realm of government. In other words, he becomes 'politicized'. This information in itself is not of much importance; but what the authors claim on the basis of this is of great consequences for students of political systems in general.

The authors argue that this process of politicization finally adds up to a picture supportive of the American regime.

> The Child is initiated into a supportive stance by what is probably high exposure to cues and messages about government, even while he is essentially unconcerned with such

3. David Easton and Jack Dennis, *Children in the Political System: Origins of Political Legitimacy* (New York, 1969).

4. *Ibid.*, p. 4.

5. *Ibid*, p. 138.

matters and too young to do much about them even if he wished.[6]

Easton and Dennis maintain that the child learns to like the government before he really knows what it is, and that as he learns what it is he finds that it involves popular participation, which is a valuable part of its countenance. It, they hold, is further reason for liking it and the child continues to like it. They conclude, "The child has somehow formed a deep sympathy for government even before he knows that he is in some way potentially a part of it."[7] The authors seem to have drawn a very one sided picture of the process of socialization of the American child. There is nothing in their argument to suggest that some children, even in America, may develop apathy toward the government. We will discuss this issue in details at a later stage. Here it is sufficient to note the conclusion drawn by Easton and Dennis.

Easton and Dennis examine the obvious question connected with this conclusion : How does the child come to acquire such knowledge and develop such sympathies ? They find that there are some authority figures which are more visible and, therefore, salient to the child. In the United States the President and the policeman are found to be two such figures. The authors hold that the child feels vulnerable to the world outside the family and these authority figures serve his immediate psychic needs.[8] On the basis of this argument they infer :

> For the political systems, however, the feelings of vulnerability that might have led him (The child) to elevate two authority figures to positions of considerable prominence have important consequences. They may help to lock the child in the political system and to provide the system with a mechanism for accompanying those kinds of sentiments without which, we have hypothesized, no system

6. *Loc. cit.*
7. *Loc. cit.*
8. *Ibid.*, p. 161.

could hope to persist, whether in constant or changed form.[9]

The survey conducted by the authors show that the child ascribes towering status and authority, and places the care of the country in the hands of the president. The authors interpret this as the latent approval of the president.[10] They find that most of these children think that the president is inherently likeable and benevolent, since he would help and protect them more often than not.[11] They, further, find that the child views the president as the living symbol of the political system. Easton and Dennis argue,

> If the president is indeed the living symbol of the political system — 'our government'—for the young child, the main conduit through which a child moves into the fuller stream of political life in the United States, we may suspect that support for the regime arises easily and naturally.[12]

One may argue that the child's approval may be based on his information about a particular president and, therefore, there is no scope for generalization about the American System But the authors point out that it is unlikely that the child has enough information about the personal qualities of a given individual to be able to make judgements about him. The children must, therefore, be making assumptions about the characteristics of all presidents as persons who hold office.[13]

Easton and Dennis call this process personalization. They maintain that personalization facilitates the development of elemental feelings like love and hate. It also incorporates a host of other attributes that children are accustomed to associating with ordinary people, such as leadership, power

9. *Ibid.*, p. 162.
10. *Ibid.*, p. 177.
11. *Ibid.*, p. 189.
12. *Ibid.*, p. 191.
13. *Ibid.*, p. 197.

and benevolence.[14] One may still doubt if this process amounts to support for a particular president. The authors dispel this doubt by stating that their "data suggest that in the United States personalization is not the same as acceptance of the legitimacy of a figure of authority on purely personal ground."[15] In personalization they claim to have tapped a major source of legitimaey for a regime. Their interpretation of the possible system-effect of personalization carries them to believe that this is a central mechanism available to many political systems for buliding up diffuse support in each wave of children.[16] They, however, note that if personalization of authority for the child is viewed as a phenomenon that is universal in character then explanation of input of support in the systems with no central personal figure in the authority structure will be problematic. They duck the issue and go on to say,

> Whatever the way in which other systems might handle the socialization of support, in the United States the president as a personalized figure is a towering glittering mountain-peak for the younger child, easy to single out from the whole range of authority.[17]

They argue that even though the older child may see authority in more critical and less enthusiastic terms, early idealization may create latent feelings that are hard to undo or shake-off. This is seen as the major significance of the first bond to the system through the presidency. "The positive feelings for political authority generated there can be expected to have lasting consequences".[18]

The other authority figure which the authors find, serving a similar purpose, is the policeman. They inquire into the

14. *Ibid.*, p. 201.
15. *Ibid.*, p. 202.
16. *Ibid.*, p. 205.
17. *Ibid.*, p. 206.
18. *Ibid.*, p. 207.

functions of the policeman as a central connecting point between maturing members of a system and the structure of polical authority. They find that the child sees the policeman as a power over and beyond that of father or mother and one that even parents cannot escape. Easton and Dennis argue that through the policeman the child is encouraged in the belief that "external authority should and must be accepted".[19] Here we must take note of the fact that socialization as a step to muster support must aim at creating a sense of legitimacy. Legitimacy can't be based on the belief that external authority should and must be accepted. Only if a sense of "ought" is cultivated can a sense of legitimacy arise.

Easton and Dennis do not use the term 'ought'. May be they actually mean ought when they say "should and must be accepted." However their data show that in the socialization process, as for the president, the child acquires feelings for the policeman that are very significant for the growth of an attachment to the structure of political authority.[20]

The authors hypothesise that if children in a particular political system confuse political and familial authority, there would be little opportunity to begin the acquisition of supportive sentiments about specific political objects.[21] Enquiring into this aspect of the question they find that the child distinguishes between these two kinds of authorities. Moreover, he gradually becomes aware of the existence of differences among political authorities.[22] They point out that the child does not consider all political authorities endowed with similar degrees of role competence. "He develops a finer level of discrimination, one that is of considerable consequences for the extension of support for these authorities".[23]

19. *Ibid.*, pp. 221-227.
20. *Ibid.*, p. 229.
21. *Ibid.*, p. 253.
22. *Ibid.*, p. 254.
23. *Loc. cit.*

This analysis leads Easton and Dennis to the conclusion that children clearly consider the existence of sharp differences, on effective and performance characteristics, between father as an authority and that kind of authority outside the family which is designated as political. Secondly, that the children differentiate among political authorities themselves. The authors find that the initial attachment of children to personal objects in the political sphere wanes across the grades and they begin to recognize political institutions.[24]

Easton and Dennis, then, link these findings to the question of system persistence. They maintain that as the child becomes aware of the structure of political authority and becomes able to relate to it in role specific terms, conditions in the system make it possible to begin to evoke diffuse support from him. At the same time as the child begins to perceive authorities beyond the small circle of family, as he becomes "politicized", he develops positive sentiments about them.[25] On the basis of this Easton and Dennis observe about the American system :

> The overwhelming thrust of primary socialization in this system must, therefore, be toward political stability. Early orientations provide a solid supportive base for the regime as the member grows older.[26]

This process through which diffuse support is stated to be built, is summarized by the authors in the concepts of personalization, institutionalization, politicization and idealization. This view holds that the child reaches out to the political system through the structures of authority and at the beginning finds palpable human objects such as the president and the policeman, and government interpreted in a personal way. His contact points are "personalized". Their data shows that the child views the president and the policeman as

24. *Ibid.*, p. 271.
25. *Ibid.*, p. 276.
26. *Ibid.*, p. 287.

benevolent. Thus the personalized authority figures are also "idealized". The child gradually begins to distinguish between the internal authority of the family and the external authority and thus become "politicized". The politicized child is capable of extending the idealized image of the personalized figures of authority to the institutions and this is designated as "institutionalization". Easton and Dennis view these processes as contributory to the process of mobilization of diffuse support for political authority. They write :

> Socialization during childhood is characterized by processes that we have labelled politicization, personalization, institutionalization, and idealization. All these processes seem to interlock in such a way as to contribute to a relatively high level of diffuse support for political authority.[27]

The authors find that these processes do not vary with variation in sex, social status and regions. They point out that they have not been able to find large, consistent differences in their data among various salient sub-categories of respondents. The differences they observe are scattered, unsystematic and more impressive for their absence than for their presence.[28] They claim to have shown that children are politically not irrelevant. They suggest that through personalization, idealization, politicization and institutionalization the child becomes a member of the political system and in becoming simply a member one of the first thing he learns to do is to extend support to (or reject in varying degrees) whatever he considers to represent the political authorities.[29] The authors identify this process as a condition for the persistence of any and all political systems. They argue,

> The burden of our analysis presses us toward the conclusion that without some means for politicizing children and

27. *Ibid.*, pp. 318-319.
28. *Ibid.*, p. 378.
29. *Ibid.*, p. 399.

> for coupling them through personalization to the structure of authority, it would be difficult to bring maturing members in most systems to accept legitimacy of the regime.[30]

Contrary to these findings a number of studies show that all American children do not idealise authority structures. Easton and Dennis are aware of this possibility. They in fact refer to one such study[31] conducted before their own study. But they maintain that even such findings do not affect their inferences about political socialization and its system effect. Because,

> for the children to develop hostility toward the authorities, it is also necessary that they became politicized enough to differentiate parental from political authority, that they make personalized contact with figures of authority so as to learn whom to hate (rather than idealize) and that they may transfer their negative effect to institutions.[32]

They have thus, broadened the meaning of politicization even to include a situation where the maturing members, instead of idealizing reject the authority figures. They thus seem to draw our attention to both the positive and negative effects of political socialization.

However, the major claim of Easton and Dennis remains that they have established the relevance of children for political science. They make this claim very clear when they say that far from simply searching for the roots of adult behaviour intuitively selected as interesting, they have laid down some theoretical criteria to guide research of primary socialization. They then ask "where have these theoretical guide-

30. *Ibid.*, p. 408.

31. D. Jaros H. Hirsch, and F. Fleron J : "The Malevolent leader: Political Socialization in an American Sub-culture" *American Political Science Review*, Vol. LXII, pp. 564-575.

32. Easton and Dennis, *op. cit.*, p. 417.

lines now led us ? They have brought us to recognize the political void, in which past research has unwittingly placed children".[33] This inference, as is evident from our discussion above, is based on their fiding that the child does personalize political authorities which in turn leads to his politicization. However, a number of studies conducted in other nations have shown that children do not always personalize political authorities of their own system. R.W. Conwell finds that in Australia such personalization is not present.[34] Jon H. Pammet has found that the American President is more familiar to Canadian children. He, further, finds that in Canada children know more about parliament than about their prime minister.[35] In the face of this evidence it is difficult to accept the conclusion of Easton and Dennis that children do personalize political authority of their own system. The question that arises is : How do Easton and Dennis arrive at this conclusion ? May be the very administration of their questionnaire has in some way stimulated such responses which show that the child personalize authority. We do not have conclusive evidence on this; but as Vaillancourt says, "it is possible that the political socialization researcher, himself, *creates* attitudes instead of measuring existing ones."[36] (emphasis added). It is possible to argue that attitudes cannot be created in this manner. However, the possibility of stimulation of a particular kind of responses cannot be ruled out. Specially in a highly competitive society like America no child would like to be known as 'not knowing' and therefore would try to respond in a manner that conforms to the 'in' ideas about authority figures.

Even if we concede that children do personalize political authorities, this personalization becomes significant only if

33. *Ibid.*, p. 388.
34. R.W. Conwell, *The Child's Construction of Politics*, (Melbourne, Australia, 1971).
35. Jon H. Pammet, "The Development of Political Orientations" *Canadian Journal of Political Science*, Vol. IV, pp. 132-141.
36. Pauline Mari Vaillancourt: "Stability of Children's Survey Responses", *Public Opinion Quarterly*, Vol. XXXVII, p. 376.

we assume that it shapes the adult behaviour. Because the persistence of a political system is dependent on the behaviour of the adult members and not of children. It is the support of the adults which determines the persistence of a system. Support indeed, is a political behaviour. Unless we assume that this political behaviour is somehow shaped by attitudes learnt during childhood, the child loses its political relevance. This assumption is inherent in the political socialization research of Easton and Dennis.

While stating the purpose of their study the authors describe the political system as an open system and then go on to say that the political system, being an open system can survive in the face of stress only if it can maintain a level of support. They clearly state "our central purpose will be to investigate how this kind of support is marshalled through the early socialization of those new to the system by virtue of their birth in it".[37] They make this assumption explicit when they say that in many areas of enquiry they may nevertheless hold to the theory that "what is learnt early in life tends to be retained and to shape later attitudes and behaviour."[38]

Easton and Dennis, however, are not the only ones to assume this. There are a host of other authors who do this. Hess and Torney, for instance, say, "the argument for the importance of childhood learning for the poli ical behaviour of adults appears to have considerable validity".[39] Siegal also supports this assumption when he writes, "Having once internalized the Society's norms it will presumably not be difficult for the individual to act in congruence with them".[40]

This assumption is, of course, only a part of a much more

37. Easton & Dennis, *op. cit.*, p. 4.
38. *Ibid*, p. 9.
39. R. Hass and J.V. Torney : *The Development of Political Attitudes in Children*, (Chicago, 1967), p. 7.
40. R. Siegal, "Assumptions About the Learning of Political Values" *Annals*, 361, (1965), p. 1.

important assumption, which, David Marsh shows to be present in all Socialization research. To quote Marsh,

> It is claimed that political socialization is an important factor, a key variable in understanding the operation of the political system. This is because political attitudes shape political behaviour and this behaviour provides the stimulus for change and the underpinning of stability. If this is the case then studying the development of political attitudes should help to explain systematic stability and change.[41]

The primary aim of Easton and Dennis is to study system persistence in a world of 'stability and change' they hope to do it (at least partially) by studying the development of basic political orientations in children. They suggest that their "study about children and their basic political orientations should help to extend our knowledge about the conditions surrounding the persistence of political systems as a class of phenomena".[42]

They cannot expect to do this unless they assume that an understanding of change and stability of political attitudes will facilitate an understanding of stability and change within the political system.

This assumption is founded on three other assumptions of which the assumption that "adult behaviour is shaped in part by attitudes learnt during childhood socialization" is one. The two other assumptions are : (1) Adult opinions are in a large part the end product of political socialization, (2) Individual political opinions (and the resulting behaviour) have an impact on the operation of a nations government and political life.[43]

41. David Marsh, "Political Socialization : The Implicit Assumptions questioned", *British Journal of Political Science*, Vol. 1, pp. 454-54.
42. Easton & Dennis, *op. cit.*, p. 6.
43. See Marsh, *op. cit.*, pp. 453-56.

The validity of these assumptions are not beyond reasonable doubt. Before we examine these assumptions individually, we must look into a general problem associated with each one of these assumptions. Findings of any study with such assumptions are based on answers received to questions which are administered in the form of questionnaires. Researchers ask questions which are expected to reveal the attitudes of the respondents. Such studies do not make distinction between express and actual attitudes. It is not necessary that express attitudes should always be actual attitudes Many situational and personal factors may compell a person to express an attitude which he may not actually hold. It seems the only way to find out whether express attitudes are also real attitudes is to study them in the light of the behaviour of the respondents. Which implies that attitudes will have to be studied with the help of behaviour. But students of socialization turn the process up side down. They want to explain behaviour with the help of what they call attitudes, which are actually express attitudes only. Express attitudes cannot help us to understand behaviour. Because such attitudes are expressed only to suit the occasion. They cannot explain the psychological process that results in a particular behaviour.

To come back to the three assumptions mentioned above. Marsh shows that there are some doubts as to the stability of personality dimensions, attitudes and behavioural intentions and as to the necessary primacy of early socialization.[44] Human attitudes and behaviour do not always tally. Personal and situational factors may always intervene between attitudes and behaviour. Kavanagh has pointed out that a major task facing researchers in the field of political socialization and culture is that of establishing linkages between attitudes and behaviour and linking these in turn to the performance of the political system.[45] There are other authors who have pointed

44. *Ibid.*, p. 459.
45. Dennis Kavanagh, "Allegiance Among English Children: A Disent", *British Journal of Political Science*, Vol. 2, (1972), p. 129.

out that there are lots of situational factors that intervene between attitudes and behaviours.[46] C. Wright Mills also pointed out the disparity between attitudes and behaviour and called it the central methodological problem of Social Sciences.[47]

Political Socialization research of Easton and Dennis, Hess and Easton and others like them, where the focus is on the attitudes of children, involves the other question : whether attitudes acquired during child childhood persist into the adulthood ? Easton and Dennis do not explicitly say that they do. They ask, "is there any evidence at all that either negative or positive orientations toward a system have their source in childhood experiences ?"[48] But the fact that they ask this question should not lead us to the belief that they do not subscribe to the view that such orientations originate in childhood experiences. Because if they do not assume that childhood attitudes persist into adulthood there will be hardly any ground to justify their own research. After all with their proclaimed interest in system-persistence why should they study childhood attitudes if they do not believe that these at itudes will effect adulthood attitudes ? In fact the subtitle of their book *Children in Political System,* itself is revealing. They call it '*an inquiry into the origins of legitimacy*'. Now, the origins of legitimacy could be found in childhood only if childhood orientations influence adult attitudes. Kavanagh has cautioned us against such an assumption.

46. See for instance A.W. Wicker, Attitudes Versus Actions: The Relationship of Verbal and Overt Behavioural Responses to Attitudes Objects", *Journal of Social Issues*, 425, (1969), 41-78 and I. Deutscher "Word and Deeds: Social Science and Social Policy", *Social Problem*, Vol. 13, (1966), pp. 235-54.

47. C. Wright Mills, "Methodological Consequences of Sociology of Knowledge" in L, Hrrowitz (ed.) *Power Politics and People: The Collected Essay of C. Wright Mills*, (New York, 1963), p. 467.

48. Easton and Dennis, *op. cit.*, p. 5.

He asserts that there is ample evidence of the non-generalization of childhood political attitudes into adulthood. He asks a pertinent question : "How is one to relate the overwhelming allegiance and favourable views which the mass of American children have of their political institutions with the wide measures of mistrust and cynicism found among adults ?"[49] There is only one reasonable answer to this questionchild - hood attitudes do not generally influence adult attitude and behaviour. In that sense studying childhood attitudes does not help us to understand adult political behaviour.

Finally, all political socialization research use quantitative material to measure individual attitudes or group attitudes. These are then used to explain the operation of the political system. Easton's work on political socialization also does this. In *The Children in Political System*, the authors deliberately exclude non-English speaking children, non-whites, pupils at private and parochial institutions, and those living outside major metropolitan areas; they study the attitudes of the white urban American Children and then try to explain how these attitudes help the system to mobilize diffuse support.[50] Hess and Easton also do the same thing when they study the child's image of the president.[51] The assumption in these works is that individual political opinions and the resultant behaviour have an impact on the nation's political life. This assumption is present in the works of other scholars also.[52] But as David Marsh has pointed out "an elementary

49. Kavanagh, "Allegiance Among English Children: A Dissent" *op. cit.*, p. 129.

50. Easton and Dennis, *op. cit.*, p. 422.

51. R.D. Hess and David Easton "The Child's Changing Image of the President", *Public Opinion Quarterly*, Vol. XXIV (Winter 1966), pp. 632-644.

52. See, for instance, R. Dawson and K. Prewitt, *Political Socialization* (Boston, 1969), pp. 41-60. E.S. Green Berg, "Consensus and Dissent Trends in Political Socialization Research" in E.S. Green Berg (ed.) Political Socialization, (New York, 1970), p. 16.

study of any nation will show that not all individuals' political behaviour and attitudes have equal influences."[53] Marsh suggests :

> bearing in mind the purpose of political socialization research we should study the behaviour (not the attitudes) of the elite (not the entire population) as their behaviour is likely to have most influence on the operation of the political system.[54]

Marsh has rightly pointed out the weaknesses of such research, but even the studies of elite behaviour do not take us very far in our bid to understand the problem of stability and change in political systems. To understand this problem we must understand what causes political behaviour and how ? It is not sufficient to study political behaviour in general. Only a study of the specific political behaviour of the politically relevant sets of people in a determinate political system can help us to understand the question of stability and change in political systems. We must understand the nature of social and political forces that produce political behaviour. It is not just the behaviour of a certain person or groups that determine the politics of a nation. Such behaviour may give a tilt here or a turn there; but the actual determinants of the politics of any nation must be sought in the prevalent social and political forces. Political behaviour is a social activity, in the sense that it takes place within a society. Such behaviour, therefore, must be studied in the context of the society in which it takes place.

In any historically determined society the material relations represent the real base and the political and the ideological relations represent the superstructure. In any society where there are antagonistic forces at work at the base level will have such forces at the level of superstructure as well. That is why we find the existence of organization and ideologies

53. Marsh, *op. cit.*, p. 456.
54. *Ibid*, p. 464.

expressing the interest of different classes and social groups within a society. The process of origin and development of social ideas is a complex one. The ideas do not come into the world as an automatic reflection of the base. Economics does not produce philosophical, religious, moral, aesthetic or political ideas. Ideas, indeed, are created by people. But they do not create them from a vacuum. These ideas are created under existing social conditions. This, however, is not to rule out the independence of the development of social ideas. Only in the final analysis are such ideas determined by the economic base. Moreover, having once arisen on a certain base, a superstructure reacts upon the base. This reaction may be very great. But the point here is that in all class societies there are antagonistic forces in that base which are also reflected in the superstructure. In other words, there is no homogenous social consciousness. All social consciousness, including those of children, are closely related to the legal and political superstructure which is founded upon the production relations. These relations of production, lead to a division of society into classes. The positions of each class and their consciousness, in the final analysis, are determined by the positions of these classes within the process of production.[55]

This, of course, is not to mean that each class has its own consciousness and is independent of the influences of the ideas of other classes. The dominant ideas of any society would definitely have a pervasive influence over the whole society. As Marx put it,

> The ideas of the ruling class are in every epoch the ruling ideas; i.e., the class, which is the ruling material force of society, is at the same time its ruling intellectual force. The class which has the means of material production at its disposal, has control at the same time over the means of mental production, so that thereby, generally speaking,

55. See George Lukacs: *History and Class Consciousness*, Rodwy Livingstone (Tr.) (London. 1971) p. 46.

the ideas of those who lack the means of mental production are subject to it.[56]

These sentences do give the impression that the ruling class has an absolute hegemony over others. But Miliband has pointed out that the ideological predominance of the ruling class may not always be equally effective.[57] The fact, however, remains that the ruling classes do have at their disposal very important means of influencing the other classes. Mass media and schooling for instance are two such means. The conditions arising out of the position of a particular class and the influences of dominant ideas of the society react with each other to form attitudes of people. Thus in any study of attitude formation the question of social conditions cannot be ignored.

Easton and Dennis are apparently aware of this fact. While trying to explain the high degree of consensus about the legitimacv of the authorities among their sample they point out that this may be a product of the special character of their sample which includes children only from "white urban areas not severely depressed economically".[58] It is, of course, clear that what they imply here does not involve any class analysis. They only seem to wonder that economic position of the children under study may have something to do with their attitudes towards political authorities. But it remains only a wondering. Because despite this realization about the limitation of their sample they do go on to generalize about the children's attitude to political authorities in America on the basis of information collected from such a sample. As a result of this they arrive at conclusions which indicate that the American political system has been able to muster sufficient support through early socialization. But in view of our discussion above this conclusion may not hold good. The only

56. K. Marx, *German Ideology*, (London, 1965), p. 60.

57. Miliband, *op. cit.*, p. 53.

58. Easton and Dennis, *op. cit.*, pp. 378-79.

legitimate conclusion that such a study may arrive at is that among the particular category of children under study the American political system seems to have been able to muster sufficient support. However, as we have shown above, socialization research of this brand, based, as they always are, on questionable assumptions, fail to fulfil their declared task of explaining how political systems manage to persist in a world of stability or of change.

CHAPTER 8

In Conclusion

This study was undertaken to assess David Easton's contribution to political science. Easton's main concern is political theory and he writes from the perspective of an American political scientist who was worried about the so called "decline of political theory". Easton maintains that as a result of this decline, American political science has failed to produce any reliable political knowledge. There cannot be any two opinions about the fact that in the fifties of this century when Easton started writing, political theory was a neglected area of study in American political science. Our analysis of the emergence and the development of political science in America in Chapter I shows that it was not merely a case of decline of political theory; there was in fact a certain casualness about the study of theory. The period of the emergence of American political science was characterized by drastic changes in American society. The emerging discipline took upon itself the task of training citizens to accept the new order and the values attached to it. The discipline went through the stages of reformism, pragmatism, scientism and behaviouralism. In each of these stages it neglected the study of political theory. The concept of decline has implicit in it the assumption that at some point in history, political theory was in a state of ascendency or was having its hey day. That, however, was not the case in the Unitep

States. Therefore, it is our contention that it was not merely a case of decline; American political science, as a discipline, never took political theory seriously.

Though we may not agree with Easton on the question of decline of political theory in America we must appreciate the fact that he puts forward a strong case in favour of the necessity of studying political theory. His argument that all mature scientific knowledge is theoretical, is valid. His persistent arguments have successfully drawn the attention of the discipline to the serious consequences of the neglect of political theory.

On the basis of these arguments Easton hopes to win back for theory its proper place in the study of political science. He seems to have achieved this goal; but his own attempt at theorization needs a close examination. In his effort at theory building Easton provides us with a general theory of politics. This theory is presented in the form of a conseptual framework which views the political life as a 'constructive system'. Now, the political system is perceived as an open, boundary maintaining, responsive system with two essential variables. The idea is that of a flow model where the system receives 'inputs' (demands and supports) from the environment and converts them to 'outputs' (decisions and actions of authorities). The consequences of these outputs are returned to the system as inputs through a feedback system. If the process works smoothly the 'essential variables' (making authoritative allocations and getting them accepted as binding) of the system remain within the 'critical range'. So long as these variables remain within the 'critical range' the system persists. Despite Easton's protestations, the 'critical range', as we have shown, is another version of the idea of equilibrium. If the flow model operates, the system is in an equilibrium. If the balance between the inputs and the outputs is disturbed as a result of the failure of the feedback, the equilibrium is lost and the system fails to persist. Easton, of course, claims that in the case of occurrence of stress, the system can take corrective steps. If such stress is the result of overflow of demands, corrective steps will be taken through the 'gate keepers'. If the stress results from the fall in support for any or all of the 'political objects' —the Authorities, the Regime and the Political community — the corrective steps will be directed towards these objects. In such a case the system may modify or change any or all of the 'political objects'.

Our analysis of Easton's ideas on political theory (Chapter II) and his conceptual framework (Chapter IV and V) reveals that in the ultimate analysis his idea of a political theory is that of a conceptual framework only. He hopes that such a framework will enable political science to produce reliable knowledge. But our analysis shows that his own framework fails to do that. We agree with Thomas Landon Thorson that Easton's framework can merely handle change; it cannot explain change. Moreover, it cannot explain why particular policies are adopted by particular governments. Thorson calls it a futile enterprise. He maintains that this futility is caused by the fact that Easton adopts the prediction-generalization model for scientific theory. This Explanation for the futility of Easton's enterprise does not, however, appear to be convincing for if it were so, systems analysis in physiology, which is also based on the same model of science, should also have been an equally futile exercise. Systems analysis in physiology is a branch of General Systems theory which itself is firmly rooted in holism. Holism believes in unity of sciences and aims at integration of scientific knowledge. An analysis of Easton's system analysis (Chapter IV) shows that he has broken away from this tradition. He uses the concept of system for an entirely different purpose, namely, to delimit the field of political science. It is this break, as we tried to show in chapter four which may partially explain why Easton's framework loses its utility.

Moreover, Easton views political life as a system *not* because he thinks that it *is* a system; but because it is *convenient* to do so. With the help of the idea of an 'analytical' political system he aims at building an all time all plac e general theory of politics. Such a theory cannot focus on any determinate political system. It focuses on 'politics in general'. While doing so, in the place of determinate, historical political systems he interpolates the idea of a political system in general. In the process, the framework becomes so general as to become a meta-theory rather than theory. The structure of this theory is so abstract that it becomes impossible to find an empirical point of reference. This exercise carries Easton's political science to the realm of metaphysics. It is no wonder that this framework fails to produce any reliable knowledge — the one purpose for which Easton had sought to develop his framework. Although Easton's exercise in theory building produces this abstract framework, yet he intended his theory to be empirical. He pleads for a theory which will be able to 'order all political data'.

To say this is by no means to imply that Easton ignores the question of values. In his book *The Political System* and also in his famous presidential address to the American Political Science Association, Easton took great pains to emphasize the role of value theory. He argues that political scientists must take a "constructive approach" to the question of values. In this approach a theorist is expected to spell out his normative preferences not only to inform others about these but also to enable himself to "check the impact of his moral views on his theory". Easton advocates the need to develop a set of theories free from the influence of the moral views of the theorist. This idea is based on the belief that it is possible to deal with facts without getting involved in normative issues. We tried to show, in Chapter II, that an attempt to develop an empirical political theory free from the value bias of the theorist would prevent political scientists from studying the really crucial issues of political and social life. Such an approach would make the study of normative questions impossible for political scientist. Even central questions of political theory like the right order of society would be placed outside the scope of political theory. By viewing political theory within these parameters Easton remains in line with the positivist tradition.

As a result of this approach to political theory Easton's political science would tend to become descriptive in nature. An analysis of Easton's definition of politics reinforces this conclusion. Easton rightly argues that the traditional definitions of politics which centred round the concepts of state and power failed to define politics. It is true that we need a definition of politics which views it as an activity and carefully demarcates it, for analytical purposes, from other related phenomena. But Easton's definition of politics as the authoritative allocation of values for a society does not serve the purpose. Evans and Vandyke are right in pointing out that the key terms in this definition are ambiguous and hence it fails to identify and define political phenomena. But the more important point to note in this connection is that such a definition casts political science in an allocative frame. As a result, like the neo-classical marginal allocative economists, political scientists of this hue prevent themselves from asking fundamental questions about the nature of political power and the related normative questions like, whether it is right, just and so on. As this definition focuses on policy decisions as allocation of values it makes it unnecessary for the political scientists to go into the 'core assumptions' of political power in any determinate society. Though it does not neglect power as such it focuses merely on the distribution of power and not on the purpose of political power. It must be noted here that the purpose of power is also a normative question and therefore, Easton's political science with its positivist roots would not permit its discussion. A political science which merely *describes* the distribution of power but does not go into the questions concerning the purpose of such distribution, loses much of its utility. Moreover, such a perspective brings a conservative bias to political theory. It remains concerned with the reality; but only as it exists. We have tried to show in chapter five that such a concern brings a status-quo bias to Easton's theory.

The status-quoist nature of Easton's theory is revealed also by the way he deals with the question of system maintenance and the roles of consensus and equilibrium in his theory.

Like all other forms of systems analysis Easton's approach also cannot avoid the issue of system maintenance. In 1957, in his first attempt to build a framework for systems analysis of political life Easton took a position which clearly reflected a maintenance bias. We have tried to show in the fifth chapter that under his framework, as spelled out in 1957, he perceived the main research task as one which sought to examine how a system maintained itself. But over a decade a shift seems to have taken place in his approach. In his works published in 1965, and after, he insists that he is concerned with 'persistence' and not 'maintenance'. Easton deliberately chooses the term persistence to refer to the continuous existence of a political system, if necessary through changes, as against maintenance which refers to keeping the political system in a certain condition. We note that most of the major criticism against the maintenance bias of the systems approach in social sciences came in late fifties. Though Easton himself was not enjoined, such criticism was forcefully directed against scholars like Talcott Parsons. In an interview with the author of the present study Easton indicated that he was aware of these criticism.[1] Therefore, the deliberate attempt on Easton's part to avoid the term maintenance seems to be intended to pre-empt such criticism. But such avoidance does not liberate his framework from its conservative bias. An analysis of the roles of consensus and equilibrium in his theory makes the point clear.

In our analysis of Easton's framework as developed in 1957 and also in 1965 and later, we have noted that equilibrium and consensus play very important roles in his framework. The idea of the critical range, as we have mentioned above, is reminiscent of the equilibrium theory and the whole political process is actually viewed as the result of a consensus. This perspective is also evident in Easton's work on political socialization, which has status-quoist implications.

In our analysis of Easton's empirical work in the area of

1. See Appendix.

political socialization we have tried to show that these studies were undertaken on the assumption that an understanding of change and stability of political attitudes of children would facilitate an understanding of stability and change within the political system. We have explained that this assumption itself was based on three questionable assumptions viz. (1) Adult behaviour was shaped in part by attitudes learnt during childhood, (2) Adult opinions were in large part the end product of political socialization, (3) Individual political opinions (and the resulting behaviour) had an impact on the operation of a nation's government and political life. We have further pointed out that these studies attempt to understand behaviour in terms of attitudes, which actually express attitudes only. These studies tend to generalize children's attitudes to the American political system on the basis of a sample collected from among white urban children in metropolitan areas. We have argued in the sixth chapter that since man's consciousness is determined to a great extent by his social existence no general conclusions could be drawn from such studies which are confined to certain strata of the society. But as in his theoretical framework, here too Easton assumes that support or oppositon to a political system is the result of a consensus among its members.

The emphasis on equilibrium and consensus reflected in Easton's political science is the outcome of his perception of reality. On the one hand reality can be viewed as pervaded by consensus with given structures, capable of experiencing only limited changes. Such a view of reality is essentially static. On the other hand, a reality can be viewed as beset with contradictions which are capable of transforming it. A theory which centres round the concepts of equilibrium and consensus has a view of reality as static.

At the beginning of this study, we stated that we would try to analyse if Easton's political theory could simplify reality so that it could be presented in a more comprehensible manner. We also proposed to analyse whether his view of reality was static or dynamic. In the course of our study we have demonstrated that in his bid to develop an all-time all-place general theory of politics he develops such an abstract framework which loses all empirical relevance. We have also found that he emphasises equilibrium and consensus and, therefore, has a static view of reality. This gives a conservative bias to his theory. We find that his conservatism is the result of his conformity with the logical positivist tradition on the question of value-relativism. This conclusion is supported by our analysis of Easton's idea of political theory and his definition of politics. These conclusions, however, do not deny Easton's contributions to the understanding of political science. Through his persistent arguments in favour of a serious study of political theory, Easton has won back for theory, what he himself called, "its proper and necessary place",[2] and this contribution itself should ensure him a prominent place among the great political scientists of our time.

2. Easton, *The Political System*, *op. cit.*, p. XV.

Appendix

SYSTEM CHANGE AND MARXISM : AN INTERVIEW WITH DAVID EASTON

(Following is the text of a recorded interview* with Professor David Easton)

Baruah : I am a student of Political Theory. Your work in the field of systems analysis is of great importance for political theory. The conceptual framework that you have developed has sparked off a controversy. Some social scientists have praised it sky high, others have called it a futile exercise. In view of this controversy I would like to discuss with you a few points which have been bothering me.

Landon Thorson says that the main problem with your framework is that it can neither explain change nor can it tell us why a particular set of policies are adopted. He then concludes that it is an exercise in futility. What is your reply to him ?

Easton : He is in error when he says that it does not deal with problems of change. Indeed it does deal with problems of change, in a very important way. In fact this conceptualization makes it impossible to deal with political systems except in terms of change. The reason why he mistakenly thinks that it does not deal with change is because he misunderstands one of the central concepts, the concept of system persistence, to

*This interview was recorded in New Delhi on 17th of February 1980.

mean system maintenance. It does not mean system maintenance. Systems persistence is instead a concept that is designed to raise the following kinds of questions : How does it come about that despite all the conflicts there are in society, every society nonetheless finds it possible to make authoritative allocations i.e., finds it possible to provide for the persistence of one or another kind of political system ? It means only that *some* kind of political system continues to exist *in* every society. The concept of persistence is intended to draw attention to thc problems that need to be addressed if we are to understand the conditions under which authoritative allocations can be provided by a society i.e., under which society can assure the persistence of some kind of political system. That's all the concept of persistence means in my conceptualization. But for a society to provide for some kind of political system (i.e. for some means of making authoritative allocations), sometimes that society may need to change that element in the political system we call its authorities. Every society changes authorities since human beings are mortal. Totalitarian societies change authorities less frequently than democratic societies. But all societies change authorities from time to time. That is one kind of change. In addition, however, for a society to provide for some means of making authoritative allocations it may also be necessary to change another aspect of the political system, called the regime. So far the French political system has had five republics, which are regime changes. In India during the emergency there was a fear that democracy would be lost and there would be a regime change. So regime change is an important characteristic of a political system if a society is to provide for the persistence of some way of making authoritative allocations.

Finally sometimes for a society to provide for authoritative allocations the political community itself may change. For example as I read in newspapers here, there seems to be some discussion as to whether Assam may not separate If Assam did separate then the Indian political community would be different after the separation from what it is now. So, separation (or irredentism, the opposite of separation) changes the character of the political community.

That is how systems analysis deals with changes of three sorts-authority change, regime change, and community change. These are simple concepts—the support is directed not to the system as a whole but to the regime, the authorities and the political community. If this support fluctuates for any one or combination of these three objects, it may lead to change in one or more of these objects.

In fact because the input of support is central for the maintenance or change of political systems the conditions of social revolution represent a main focus of interest for systems analysis. Revolutions are mechanism through which societies have on occasion in the past provided for some alternative means of making authoritative allocations thereby providing for the persistence (continued existence) of some kind of political system for the given society.

That is why it puzzles me when people who read systems analysis say that it does not deal with change. Change is in fact the central issue. That is the central problem. It is true that sometimes a regime may maintain themselves. Systems analysis, since it tries to be comprehensive, deals with the problems of system maintenance as well as system change. System persistence does not mean system maintenance exclusively nor does it mean system change exclusively. All that the idea of system persistence does is to pose the question : How does it come about that in every society some means are provided for making authoritatives allocations. The means that are provided may be through maintenance of a given regime, authorities or political community, or it may be through the change of a given regime, authorities or political community. Only if a person failed to read my publications carefully could he conclude that my conceptualization has difficulty in dealing with change.

Baruah : I, by and large, agree with what you have to say

against Thorson, but what bothers me is the last kind of change, when you talk of the three components of political system—the authorities, the regime and the political community and the possibilities of their undergoing changes—I can visualize the possibilities of change of authorities and the regime, but in the case of political community there are difficulties. As was pointed out in a review of your book *A Systems Analysis of Political Life*, the kind of examples you give refer to situations where a particular part of the political community goes away or somebody comes and joins ; but that is not the sense in which you are talking of changes when you refer to authorities and the regime.

Easton : No it is a different kind of change. It is an important different kind of change.

Baruah : Then what is non-persistence ?

Easton : Under conditions where the political community has changed, then the society in question has revealed that it could no longer provide for an integral political system. Presumably, the system breaks up into two or more societies which, individually, come to provide separate political systems. Obviously, in not providing for an integral part of a whole political system—the political community—that society has, as an individual entity, ceased to exist. To this extent, the system has undergone both a failure of maintenance and a failure to persist. So, it is indeed a different kind of change from the change of regime and political authorities and it is because of these significant differences that I draw attention to it.

Political scientists historically have dealt with these three kinds of changes, but have not seen them systematically and tried to group them together to show their place in a theory of politics. So what I have done is sought to focus attention on all aspects of political change rather than on the ones that most political scientists are concerned about, viz : the political authorities and sometimes the regime. Let me direct your attention to a passage in *The Political System*. I think it appears somewhere around pages 40 or 50 of the book. There I have criticised political scientists—("*Political System*" was written in 1953 when I was just about your age. I had just finished my graduate course. It was the first systematic thinking I did about political science). There I accused political science of being confined to the study of the status-quo i.e. status-quo oriented. It devoted itself too ardently to system maintenance analysis. Political science in the United States (and in many other parts of the world) even to this day is largely concerned with the status-quo. Change is a peripheral interest. Now why do I say that ? That is because they are interested not in systems—politics but in allocative politics. Are you familiar with the distinction I make between the two.

Baruah : Yes, I am.

Easton : Allocative politics takes a regime as given. We have a regime in the United States—a bourgeois democratic regime—a constitutional order and constitution etc. What are most American political scientists interested in ? They are more interested in the way in which policies are made, how the authorities change, how support of various political parties varies, how pressure groups modify policies, how different parts of the electorate are able to convince the authorities to modify their policies, how parties are formed, how administrative services are organised to implement policies, how elections for authorities are organized and won, and so on. There are all problems regarding the status-quo. The maintenance of American political institutions is taken for granted as a good with the needs for only minor modifications. There are few American political scientists who are interested in the conditions under which people are dissatisfied with the regime try to change the regime and in what direction the regime may change. Systems analysis says that these are important area of research. As a result of the counter-culture movement—you know about the students revolution in 1960's and 70's—Vietnam and Watergate, among other things, a lot of Ameriean peope became disillusioned with the political authorities. They have lost some of their confidence in political authorities. The authorities have lost some of their legitimacy—their belief in their right to rule has diminished. I do not think we have seen the end of this yet. This decline in the support for the authorities may spill over to the regime—we cannot be sure but if it does it could make it easy for some political leader, who wants to move in an authoritarian direction, to change the regime.

In relationship to my work in this area a committee was set up that met for about two years in a number of conferences to study changes in alienation and support in the U.S. Some important ideas have emerged out of that. I mention this to indicate that what has happened in the U.S. in the area of increasing alienation has led some people to turn to systems analysis to find a set of categories that might shed some light on this new and unexpected phenomenon called political alienation. Some of them have found assistance in the concept of input of support. In this way systems analysis has provided already-made conceptualization of how to understand and interpret theoretically some new and simple facts in the political life of the U.S.

What this change in level of support raises, from a systems point of view, is whether the alienation (declining input of support) from the authorities if it continues long enough, could not spill over into loss of trust and confidence in the regime, or even the political community. At least one study of migration out of the U.S. is under way which may shed some light on whether there has been some spillover to the political community. At any rate these would represent three different kinds of changes. If the political community was not able to retain the support of the American people, clearly the change this would bring about would be very different from change in the authorities and regime. But because of this very fact I have found it not only useful but necessary to build the idea into my conceptualization.

Baruah : It is clear that you distinguish between maintenance and persistence. You have explained that systems analysis is not maintenance oriented ; but do you think that in your 1957 essay, your first attempt at developing a framework for systems analysis, there was an emphasis on maintenance ?

Easton : I have not read that article for a long time. So I am not very certain whether there is or is not an emphasis on maintenance. I will have to re-read it. It is quite possible that in that article there is some such emphasis. It has been re-printed in perhaps close to a hundred different publications. So if you are right I will be glad that you are bringing it to my notice because it misrepresents my point of view.

Baruah : I have read it very carefully and I have found that at that particular stage you were perhaps not very careful about the idea of maintenance. What has happened is that when you talk of political socialization (you call it politicization) in that article and when you discuss support there is a lot of emphasis on maintenance in that article. You define political system as a process which converts inputs into outputs. Then you say that the particular research task in that particular area is to see how these processes are maintained. Now, if the process means political system and if research task is identified as inquiry into maintenance of such process then there is a clear emphasis on maintenance of the system.

Easton : Yes, that is quite possible. Perhaps, I had at that stage, not yet selected the concept of persistence. That was a deliberate choice at one point in order to discriminate between maintenance and change and finally, develop what I thought was a neutral concept that is capable of dealing with the following problem : how does it happen that a society is able to provide some means of making authoritative allocations. That is what persistence means. I regret that I chose the concept persistence becanse it is so easily confused with maintenance. And yet in the English language there is little other choice. However, the important thing is not to concentrate too much on the words. What is important is the meaning.

Baruah : Immediately after 1957 there appeared a lot of literature which attacked the status-quo bias of systems analysis. In sociology this attack was directed against Talcott Parsons, Barrington Moore and C. Wright Mills published two important books. Did you come across these books and see that unless you were very careful about the concept of maintenance it might have a status-quo bias ?

Easton : Now, I was of course, familiar with Talcott Parsons' work and also with the criticism of Parsons ; but these did not influence my thinking of systems analysis because Talcott Parsons' conception of system is quite different from mine. Unless one bears that difference in mind one would very easily ministerpret my work as having the same system maintenance bias as that of Talcott Parsons. I think many of the people who have criticised systems analysis for having a system maintenance disposition are really transposing their perception of Parsons to my work. So, therefore, the important thing is to see the difference between Parsons and Easton, and in fact if I had talked here today as I had planned, a part of my talk would have gone into an analysis of Parsons' work and its difference from mine. This would help solve the problem of misconception.

There are three stages in Parson's thinking. There is his action theory stage where he deals atomistically with the individual with a certain voluntarism that lies in the situation in which the individual acts. He tries to define what the situation is —what conditions constitutes constraints of action such as the well known five, then four pattern variables.

At a later stage he seems not to abandon this action oriented analysis but to move toward a new and different form of analysis and still later he puts these two forms of analysis together. The second stage is where he moves explicitly to a systems orientation. He moves to that stage after systems analysis became a more prominent way of thinking in the whole intellectual world. So he was influenced by this trend. But his systems thinking from the very beginning was dictated largely by his experience as an economist. He was trained initially as an economist. Like most economists he looks at economic life as a system. Like most economists he concerns himself with the problem of equilibrium, how a systems moves to and away from an equilibrium. Therefore, when he thought of the society in this particular systems framework, he decomposed society into four systems, represented by the acronym AGIL. There are four systems, they interact with each other and there are various forms of interaction. Therefore they are an interactive system, and through this interaction they function so as to meet the major needs for the maintenance of the social system called society. That is the basis of his status-quo orientation. He wants to know what the conditions are for the interactions among these four sub-system have to do to perform their function for the maintenance of a society. Systems analysis does not look at systems as interactive sub-systems. It looks at systems dynamically a special kind of dynamics. It sees a system, such as a political system, as a set of behaviours that is doing something, that produces something, that produces outputs. It produces these outputs not out of nothing but out of something, inputs. Therefore, the inputs are very important for understanding outputs. The processes – the internal processes of the system, the black box, is very important, because that is what grinds out these processes. So therefore, we look at a political system as a process, through which something is put into the system and that changes what comes into the system to something else. It is a productive system. It is not a system that is just composed of sub-systems that act and react with each other. They do that of course. But they do more. They transform what goes in into something new. They are transformational systems.

We have to look at politics as a set of internal processes that does something for us. What does it produce ? How does it produce ? What effect must support have ? What effect must outputs have ? Systems analysis has quite a different orientation from the way in which Parsons uses the idea of change, as I have already suggested. Change is central to the problems with which systems analysis deal. Although Parsons tries to show in his later works that change is a problem that he is able handle, his conceptualization makes it more than a little difficult to deal with. But even if he does handle the problem of change, systems analysis deals with it in a very different way as I have already explained.

Baruah ; Now since you have mentioned equilibrium—I thought I would ask this question at a later stage but now since you have referred to it I will ask it now. When you criticise the equilibrium concept you point out the difficulties involved in quantification...

Easton : You have read my article on equilibrium ?

Baruah : Yes, I did. You referred to the difficulties which are involved and also, though you do not discuss it in details, you definitely referred to the kind of bias that this kind of analysis may betray. Now you are saying Parsons' idea of a social system also has the bias and therefore it becomes maintenance oriented. But there is at least one point where your model also makes use of the equilibrium concept. When you talk of the critical range within the two essential variables must be kept, if the system has to persist, you are maintaining that if the essential variables are pushed beyond the critical range the system gets disturbed. I feel that the idea of the critical range is reminiscent of the equilibrium model.

Easton : There you need to recall what the critical variables refer to. The critical variables do not refer to the regime or the authorities or the political community. That is to say, they do not refer to the political system and therefore they could have little relevance to the equilibrium of this system. The critical variables refer to what ? They refer not to the political system but to society—they refer to the capacity of the society to provide (1) for the making of decisions, and (2) for getting them accepted as binding. So they are really the sociological basis of the political system. What we are saying there is that if a society cannot provide for the making of decisions or for having them accepted as binding then that society will not be able to provide for any kind of political system—whether it is a self-maintaining system or rapidly changing system, a system in or out of equilibrium if we were to even consider using such a term. Therefore if it cannot provide for any political system the society itself will collapse. So it raises a different order of problems from problems of system maintenance or equilibrium of a political system itself.

The problem it raises is a historical one which unfortunately political scientists have seldom dealt with and the historians have dealt with only partially and not consistently. The problem it raises is : To what extent does the survival of a society or the change of a society depend upon the capacity of that society to provide for some kind of political system ? For example did the Holy Roman Empire or did the old Greek city states disappear because of the failure of their economy ? Did they disappear because of the failure of their culture ? Or did they disappear because of what the historians call the failure of leadership, perhaps of the political leadership ? If they disappeared because of the failure of the political leadership, then we have to ask : What aspect of leadership ? The failure to make decisions ? Sometimes the society may be paralysed—it cannot make decisions. Or having made the decisions could it disappear because the leadership, which is to say, the authorities, were incapable of getting the members to accept the decisions as binding. Consequently, chaos, disorder, or whatever you like to call it sets in.

That is the problem that is raised by that level of conceptualization. It is a problem different from the ones encountered in those instances in which the fundamental capability of a society to provide for a political system is not in question. In these latter instances, we might ask : Is this regime showing a capacity to maintain itself amid change ? Is that regime disposed to change rapidly as a consequence of some structural features ? And so on, covering all the relevant issues.

The point I am trying to make is that my critics fail to

discriminate between the sociological problem of how a *society* provides for its own continuation and the role the political systems plays in that, and the political problems with which we as political scientists are concerned, namely, how does a *political system* manage to change or maintain itself ?

Baruah : If I understarnd you properly, are not talking of any particular political system like the Indian or the American political system. You are talking of the capacity of a society to authoritatively allocate values. Therefore your reference point is any and all societies. You are talking in terms of a universal category. You are thinking of politics in general and not of politics of a particular political system. Therefore, even if you talk of maintenance—you do not talk of maintenance, you talk of persistence—but even if you talk of maintenance it would not be the same kind of maintenance as that of Talcott Parsons. You seem to be talking of the maintenance or persistence of a process of politics.

Easton : I would avoid the word maintenance. I want to use the word persistence technically for the political processes of society, and would reserve the word maintnance to mean the continuity of the regime or authorities or the political community.

Baruah : I can see that persistence is a broader category. With this category you are referring to a different level. You are arguing that because of this difference in the level of reference the ideas of critical range and persistence become general in nature. In fact as I pointed out earlier your idea of the political system refers to the political processes itself.

Easton : Within society. So it is a sociological level that is being dealt with. That is the assumption, the basis upon which one builds a theory of politics. You cannot think of politics in a social vacuum.

Baruah : That is very important and that is where I disagree with Thorson and also Meehan to some extent. But

Meehan has pointed out something more interesting. He says that though you are dealing with politics in general, though you are trying to build a theory—a general theory of politics —what you have in your mind is probably a nation-state, a national political system. I know that you would say that you do not have the national political system. I know that you would say that you do not have the national political system in your mind when you talk of the political system. Meehan has not shown how his contention could be justified ; but when I read Meehan and referred to your *A Framework of Political Analysis* and *A Systems Analysis of Political Life*, I found that at least at one point the idea of the national political system came into picture as the basis of your framework. That was the only point where it happened in these two works. That particular point was when you discussed boundaries and environment. I understand that when you write a voluminous book like the *SAPL* some points may not receive sufficient amount of care. Maybe you consider these points minor; but later on those may become very important sources of criticism. To come back to the point, you wrote that there were two environments—intra-societal and extra-societal. Systems which are not political but within the same social system are in the intra-societal environment and the systems which are outside the social system are in the extra-societal environment of the political system under study. You have referred to the international society as being in the extra-societal environment of the political system. In that crse you are equating the political system with the national political system. Meehan probably had this in mind when he criticised you in these lines. Do you have something to say about this ?

Easton : What you say is perfectly correct...when you write a large volume it is possible sometimes for a certain phrase or paragraph to slip in with potential interpretations of which yov may not be totally aware. So I again will have to re-read this in order to clarify for myself as to whether indeed I have misrepresented my own position, accidentally. However, without having re-read that particular passage, I would say that that passage would be equally applicable to a society that had no geographic boundaries. Let us take a Bedouin tribe in Arabia somewhere before the present nation-state Saudi Arabia took shape. It would be a tribal group that would have a political system and since it was nomadic and trevelled from place to place it had no geographic boundaries. Such a system has an internal environment. This internal environment would certainly include a primitive form of economy, for every society includes processes of material production and acquisition. It would also include a system of meanings —symbolic meanings—which we would call a cultural system, and which anthropologists would insist on distinguishing from the political system. So It had at least three internal systems, each of which interacted with and influenced the others. It had an external environment too, other nomadic tribes which also perhaps had no geographic boundaries. If you are not to use that term—external systems—you would need some other term to refer to them. They are part of the international environment of other nomadic tribes, if you wish. The point is that even systems that have no geographic boundaries, such as nomadic systems, *do* have an international environment by which they may be influenced. I presume so, at least. Therefore the vocabulary I use is not only applicable to the nation-state but also to political systems that cannot be called nation srates.

Baruah : I would like to direct your attention to the distinction that you have drawn between the constructive and the natural system. You point out the difficulties of using the natural system concept and then argue that the constructive system concept avoids certain very unnecessary disputes like deciding whether a particular system is really a system or not. This dispute, according to you, may become interminable. Therefore, to avoid this you use the concept of constructive system. In this approach the only thing that engages our attention is whether a system is interesting in the sense that it enables us to understand something theoretically relevant. Do you not think that even a dispute over theoretical relevance of a system may also become interminable ?

Easton : It might; but I think in practice that it does not. If I say that I am going to be interested in the following kinds of political system—a system that comprises the people of the city of Moscow, the people of Quebec and the people of the Louisiana. If I pick up the Problems of these three Political units and say that they are a system, a constructive system, and I am interested in their Political interactions. I think most people would agree that it is an uninteresting combination of people—an uninteresting *Political* combination. It is true that in some very remote sense they may have some influence on each other, so remote that it may well be impossible to really detect it. Obviously at the extreme we will have no difficulty in excluding those arbitrarily selected systems that are of little interest and therefore, are trivial from the point of view of political theory. The fact is that if we come down to day-to-day occurrences most political scientists would agree that India is an interesting political system, that Pakistan is an interesting political system, that Bangladesh is an interesting political system and so on. In the abstract one could think that one could get into an interminable dispute, and perhaps there are some very special cases where indeed one could dispute the matter. But in most cases it is not difficult for political scientists to decide what constitutes an interesting political system and what constitutes a trivial one.

Baruah : Here may I direct your attention to the responsive nature of the political system? I have a quotation from *A Framework of Political Analysis* where you say that the political system is a goal-setting, self-transforming and creatively adaptive system. It consists of human beings who are capable of anticipating, evaluating and acting constructively to prevent disturbances in the system. It is very interesting way of putting it. Do you think that you are giving a free hand to the members of the system to decide the fate of the system ? Do you not visualize situations in which the members may know that they need to take certain decisions to prevent disturbances but they find it impossible to do so. In this sense a political system cannot be a self-regulating, adaptive system.

Easton : But if you read me carefully—I hope I am sufficiently precise to say what I mean—you will understand that, when I argue that a political system is capable of orienting itself, the question of whether, as an empirical fact, a *particular* system does so operate, is an open one. Sometime the feedback may be completely cut-off, for example, in certain periods in the history of Germany there is very little feedback. That is the problem. A dictatorial system cuts off feedback so it becomes increasingly unstable and pressure builds up underneath. In Stalin's Soviet Union, the terror led to the near failure of the regime. So the mere fact that a political system is *capable* of goal-setting, self-regulating etc. does not mean that it would in fact engage in such behaviour. That is a different question. Furthermore the fact that a system responds or seeks to regulate itself is no evidence that it will do so successfully in terms of an observer's criteria or that, given the circumstances, (such as the dropping of powerful atom bombs) it can ever do so.

Baruah : But in spite of your careful explanation that the political system may have these capacities but it may not be possible for it to utilize them—that the feedback may fail—the implications remain the same. If in a particular political system the feedback operates properly it would be possible for the members to take steps to enable the system to continue. The system would not fail.

Easton : No, that is not what I intended. We have to distinguish between two things. One is the maintenance of the system, of the regime, of the authorities...

Baruah : I am not talking of the regime and the authorities at the moment I am talking of the system...

Easton : No, there is no such implication in at least what I intend to say. Because even though there is feedback, and even though the goals may be changed, societies can make mistakes and the feedback may be misunderstood and the decision makes may choose improper goals. They may not have the resources—there are many things that could happen that could lead to the collapse of the system and the collapse of the society. So they may make a decision to use nuclear energy and ultimately destroy themselves—all kinds of bad decisions can be made.

Baruah : You are attributing it to human error...

Easton : It may be human error ; but it could be other things as well. In addition to human error it could be the exhaustion of one's resources or it could be failure to reproduce themselves. So there may not be human error. It may be the incapacity to deal with certain problems ; for example, a society may through its decisions, create a situation in which there are so many crises that it can no longer deal with these crises and the society just blows up. Well you can call that human error. Or it could be inability to cope with certain kinds of issues such as air pollution that ultimately suffocates us all ?

Baruah : Thank you Professor Easton. May I now draw your attention to the debate that is going on for sometime in many branches of social sciences, especially in social analysis, about two different madels of society ? One is called the consensns model and the other is known as the conflict model. In view of this controversy do you think that your framework might be put into either the conflict or the consensus model ?

Easton : People who read my work...

Baruah : Dahrendorff, for instance.

Easton : Yes ; people who read my work without care some times contend that I have adopted a consensus model because they see my work as moving towards system maintenance. They misconstrue system persistence to mean system maintenance. However, a careful reader would see that my work shares the same premises as those of Hobbes and Karl Marx. Both of them use a conflict basis for their work. Mine shares deliberately and explicitly the same premises that Hobbes and Marx employ. Why do I say that ? Hobbes starts off with the assumption that the state of nature is a war of all against all. That men value safety and, therefore, that they are willing to do whatever is necessary to survive—even to support a dictator. He sees the world as based on conflict—and that is precisely why you need to think of some kind of social order. Marx starts by seeing historical social organizations—primitive salavery, feudalism, capitalism, so on—as based upon exploitation—conflict among social classes. I see the basis of society as based on the existence of scarcity, of some of our valued things, whether it be fresh air, clean water, money, property, material gain, prestige, or whatever you consider valuable. There is scarcity in most areas. Therefore, these is conflict over that scarcity. The conflict may be individual, may be class based, may be ethnic in character, or it may be linguistically based, and so on. Therefore the fundamental premise of my work includes the notion of conflict. If you had total cooperation, total consensus, it would mean there would be no need for politics, no need for authoritative allocations. Politics would have no meaning. If everything took care of itself automatically the world would be what philosophical anarchists view as the ultimate millenium. You know philosophical anarchism says, following Rousseau and Proudhon, that if you educate people well euough everybody will do what is good for himself and herself and that will also be good for the society. It is the ideal that lies behind the free-market economy of Adam Smith's invisible hand. Tnat is the ideal also behind philosophical communism. That is not my image of the world. Maybe some day, a hundred thousand years from today, human beings will be of that sort. It is a nice image to have ; but in fact realities must be based on the continuation of conflict. So how can any one say that I have a consensus model ? It is a conflict model.

Baruah : Since you have brought in Marx—there is a very interesting development taking place among the Soviet social scientists. You must have seen the book *The Systems Theory*. The authors of this book say that Marxism is the best systems model. I personally feel that there is a difficulty in making such a claim. Do you think that the general systems theory (they are talking of the GST not of your kind of systems analysis) could be fitted into the Marxist framework ?

Easton : Well, they are also talking of my systems analysis. Because, although I have not read that book, some of the Marxists in Calcutta showed me a copy of it. They also showed me a criticism that some of the writers in the U.S.S.R. have made of my work especially about the concept of authoritative allocation of values, without citing me but using my ideas... I have travelled in the Soviet Union and the socialist block countries such as Czechoslovakia, Poland, Hungary etc. So I am familiar with their thinking. Many are very favourably disposed towards my thinking. In Rumania they have (or had) a systems institute, for instance. As I understand it they are bringing out, or have brought out a book, under the name something like *Great Political Thinkers* of our Day, in which they have one book which is a collection of my works. I mention it, immodestly, only to show that there is some sympathy for the systems point of view. In Czechoslovakia and Poland they are familiar with my work also. I myself have always taken the position that Marxism is a subset of systems thinking. It is one form of systems thinking. But systems analysis is more comprehensive than Marxism. Why do I say that ? I say that because Marxism sees a political system as being determined by the mode of production. To use Althussar's phrase, Marxism sees the political system as being determined by the mode of production which in turn is by the economy in the determined last instance...

Baruah : In the ultimate analysis.

Easton : Yes, in the ultimate analysis. Therefore, it has a view that the economic system is the final determinant of the political system. That kind of perspective in Marxism I say makes it a subset of systems analysis. Because within the framework of systems analysis it would be perfectably acceptable, if one were so inclined, to conclude that the political system is, perhaps, under some circumstances, determined by the economy. But in other circumstances it would be equally understandable to conclude, on the basis of evidence, that the political system is largely determined by the cultural system, by the personality system or by the religious system. Which is the determinant in the last instance ? I really do not understand that phrase. Perhaps no one understands it. I do not think even Althusser really understands it. But the economy need not always be the major determinant, if that is what the phrase means. I do not think even Marx believed it—but that is subject to discussion and dispute. In so far as one decides that the economy is really the determinant in the last instance, that is one possible conclusion consistent with a systems perspective. It would, therefore, make it plausible to see that kind of Marxism as a subset of systems analysis. I have Marxist friends with whom I have discussed this question as well as with Marxists in India and elsewhere. They are somewhat shocked to hear that Marxism can be viewed as a subset of systems theory. In fact, however, I think it should not come as a shock to some one who reads Marx. Because Mars—in this I agree with Althusser, Poulantzas and with structural Marxists in general—does indeed think in systems terms. Marx was to my mind one of the great social geniuses of all time. He organized his thinking so that he saw other aspects of society in the same way in which he saw the economy. So he was already thinking in system terms. But he did not have the vocabulary or the benefit of a great deal of additional thinking that has gone on in the hundred and so years since he died. Therefore, even though systems thinking is implicit in the way in which he organized his work, nevertheless it is just a beginning. Since Althusser and Poulantzas are products themselves of the systems revolution of our own day, in effect they interpret Marx to accommodate him to our time—to bring his thinking into a line with Twentieth Century systems analysis and hence to make Marx a little bit more modern than Marx himself could possibly have been. He was after all thinking in the nineteeth century. Althusser's three levels or instances of modes of productions—the economic, political and ideological (cultural)—are simply three major subsystems of social systems For the Althusserians, mode of production is equivalent to social system, instance or level, to subsystem, and social formation, to a concrete society. The parallel in terminology is just too close to be called accidental. And if you read Poulantzas carefully—he translates Althusser's philosophy into political sociology—you will see that in each succeeding book, he, Poulantzas, increasingly uses the concept of political system itself. So in that sense they update Marx and therefore reformulate Marx's ideas in systems terms. That is the historic role of structural Marxism.

Baruah : As I was saying I find it rather difficult to accept the kind of claims that are being made by the Soviet social scientists regarding the relationship of the Marxist mode of social analysis and the General Systems Theory and systems analysis. My difficulty is this—one of the basic things in Marxism is dialectics. Dialectics has to be understood in terms of a continuous process. A continuity which pervades the reality. You cannot isolate the economic reality, or political reality from the whole social reality. Dialectical Materialism takes the whole reality into consideration. But as V.L. Allen has pointed out, in the systems approach you try to abstract parts of social reality into small sub-systems. When one system is under study the rest of the systems from the environment. In the process, at least at the conceptual level, you break the reality into systems, sub-systems etc. Allen points out that in dialectical Materialism you cannot do that, you cannot divide society into sub-systems. If you do that you are going against Marxist.

Easton : There are two problems here. One is that—if that is his position—he has misconstrued the nature of general systems theory. What differentiates systems analysis from General Systems Theory (G.S.T.) is that General Systems Theory does not decompose reality into a series of sub-systems, looking at each sub-system in isolation as it were, as they interact with other sub-systems. Rather General Systems Theory takes as its objective the understanding of the laws that govern the operation of all systems. Therefore, it says that you have to look at the world as composed of increasingly broader systems. So you start with the sub-atomic system. You go to the atomic systems. You rise up to another level, to them olecular system, to the cellular system, to the organic system, the social system, ultimately to the galactic system perhaps. Then you look at each system and you see whether there are laws or generalizations that apply at each level and that are equally true across all levels. You are looking for the laws of all system, that is, G.S.T. There is no question that is General Systems Theory. The minute you talk of decomposing systems and seeing the ways one subsystem interacts with other subsystems you are moving either to the Parsonian model, a non-dynamic, non-feedback analysis, or you are moving to a dynamic systems analysis. Allen does not seem to be dealing with G.S.T. He is dealing either with the Parsonian model or with systems analysis. I do not know, I have not read him.

Secondly, it is perfectly true that Marxism deals with, to use the nineteenth century term, social formations. In our terms today a social formation would be called a particular society at a given time and place, conceived as a unit. One of the problems that Marxism faces today is the difficulty of creating a Marxist social science different from normal or conventional, what they would call positivistic bourgeois, social science. As some Marxists themselves say, they are in a state of crisis in this area. They have not been very successful in developing a Marxist social science. To be a social science it is not sufficient to be able to have this generalized conception of the social formation in which all parts are dialectically interconnected, in which the internal contradictions of the whole system lead to the generation of a whole new social formation. That is a theoretical formulation ; but one cannot do research on that basis alone to discover what part the political system plays in this transformation. If the political system does have some degree of autonomy, as the Althusserians argue, what part does ideology play ? Marx saw that the ideology may have some degree of autonomy too. Gramsel of course made a big issue of that and of other aspects of that assertion, in order to be able to show that each of the parts of the social formation leads to the grand contradictions which transform the whole society. You have got to be able to work out the details. Marx spent twenty years, in the British Museum for the most part, working out the details of the economy. He dealt with the other parts of the "social formation" but only in bits and pieces as for example, in connection with social classes, in a few pages at the end of the last volume of *Capital*. Contemporary serious Marxist social scientists say we have got to show what part the political system plays. Poulantzas was a serious Marxist social scientist. He was trying to work out what he called 'A Theory of the State', that is, a political theory. He was having eonsiderable difficulties. He was accused by Miliband of structural superdeterminism. But you know, all social scientists have problems. So he had his own problems too. But, the important issue is that the minute you begin to develop a Marxist social science you have to decompose the social formation into its elements. For Poulantzas and Althusser these elements or "instances" were the ideological system, the economic system, and the political system i.e. the state. The minute you begin to think about the social formation in serious terms, to see the relationship among the parts today, you are likely to turn to a systems mode of analysis. Why ? Because social scientists, today, when they begin to think in general theoretical terms, are highly likely to be affected by the systems revolution of our age. In the nineteenth century, when Marx thought about society, he was influenced by the Darwinian revolution, and social change, in Darwinian terms, is a conflictual process. In the seventeenth century when Hobbes and Locke talked about society they talked about it as though it were some giant mechanism, a clockwork. Their interpretation was shaped by the Newtonian mechanics, the revolution in thought of that century. As I have suggested not even the Marxists have been able to escape the pervasive influence of the idea of system which is so prevalent in all areas of thought in our own day. Poulantzas and Althusser have accommodated themselves to that mode of thinking. Whether they recognize it or not does not matter.

Baruah : I have forgotten to ask you another question about this holistic idea—your view of the society and of the universe is not exactly like the holistic view. Do you think that this difference has any consequence for the results of your analysis or to put it in other words will the results of analysis vary in case of application of the holistic G.S.T. to political science and system analysis ?

Easton : I am not sure of the difference you are refering to.

Baruah : The G.S.T. believes in holism. You do not. There is a difference of premises. Holistic approach tries to build a total view. It does not isolate one social phenomenon or one system from the rest. Your writing in *The Political System* makes it clear that you wanted to isolate the political system and the political phenomena for the purposes of study. Holism does not permit this. Years is a different approach.

Easton : I am sympathetic to G.S.T. Perhaps some day we may be able to discover a way of understanding politics as part of a General Systems Theory. Today, it seems to be very premature. They have my belssings. It is not something I think I can comfortably spend my time on. It boggles the mind to think of a theory that would be equally valid for all systems, from the smallest subatomic particle, up through the atom as a system, molecules, cells, organisms, groups, societies, the world society and even intergalactic systems ! I find it difficult enough to try to encompass the political system within one conceptual scheme, let alone trying to add to my troubles by including all other systems physical and biological as well as social.

The interview ended abruptly because Professor Easton became inaudible because of laryngitis. It was indeed very kind of Professor Easton that he talked to me though his voice was giving out.

———

Bibliography

Allen V.L., *Social Analysis: A Marxist Alternative*, (Longman, London, 1975).

Almond G. and Coleman J., *Politics of Developing Areas* (Princeton University Press, Princeton, New Jersey, 1960),

Almond, Gabriel A., "A Developmental Approach to Political Systems" *World Politics*, Vol. 28, No. 2, (1965) pp. 183-214.

Almond Gabriel A., "Political Theory and Political Science" *American Political Science Review*, Vol. LX (1966) pp. 869-879.

Applebaum, R., *Theories of Social Change* (Markham Publishing Co., Chicago, 1970).

Bachrach Peter and Barotz, Morton S. *Power and Poverty, Theory and Practice*. (Oxford University Press, New York, 1970).

Barry Brian, M., *Political Argument* (Humanities Press, New York 1965).

Beard Charles, E. *An Economic Interpretation of the Constitution of the United States*, (Macmillan, New York 1913).

Bell Roderick, Edwards David V and Harrison Wagner (eds.), *Political Power; A Readcr in Theory and Research*; (The Free Press, New York, 1919).

Bently A.F., *The Process of Government* (Princeton Press, Bloomington 1949).

Bernard Barber (ed.), *L.J. Handerson on the Social System: Seletced Writings*, (Chicago University Press, Chicago, 1970).

Bernard L.L. in Seligman Edwin R.A.; (ed.) *Encyclopedia of Social Sciences* Vol. II, pp. 324-249 (McMillan and Co., New York, 1957).

Bertalanffy Ludwing Von, *General Systems Theory Foundations, Development, Applications* (Brazillier, New York, 1968).

Bharadwaj Krishna, *Classical Political Economy and Rise to Dominance of Supply and Demand Theories*, (Orient Longman, New Delhi, 1978).

Blauberg I.V., Sadovsky V.N. Yudin E.G., *Systems Theory* (Progress Publishers, Moscow, 1977).

Bottomore, T.B., *Sociology on Social Criticism* (Pantheon Books, New York, 1974).

Bottomore, T.B., *Critics of Society* (George Allen and Unwin Ltd., London, 1967).

Bottomore Tom, *Marxist Sociology* (The Macmillan Press, London, 1975).

Brecht Arnold, *Political Theory: The Foundations of Twentieth Century Political Thought*, (The Times of India Press, Bombay, 1965).

Compbell, C.S.J., "Current Models of the Political System: An Intellective Purpose View", *Comparative Political Studies* 4, (1971), pp. 21-40.

Canon W.B., *Wisdom of the Body* (Norton, New York, 1963).

Catlin G.E.G., *A Study of the Principles of Politics* (George

Allen and Unwin, London, 1930).

Catlin G.E.G., *Science and Methods in Politics*. Knopf, New York, 1927).

Catlin G.E.G., *Systematic Politics* (University of Toronto Press, Canada, 1962).

Charlesworth, C. (ed.), *Contemporary Political Analysis*, (Free Press, New York, 1967).

Cobban Alfred, *In Search of Humanity*, (Brazillier, New York, 1960).

Cobban Alfred, 'The Decline of Political Theory', *Political Science Quarterly*, Vol. LXVIII (September, 1953), pp. 321-337.

Cohen, P.S.. *Modern Social Theory* (Heinman Educational Books Ltd., London, 1968).

Collingwood, R.G., *Essay on Philosophical Method* (Oxford University Press, Cambridge, 1953).

Converse Philip, Book Review, *American Political Science Review* Vol. LIX No. 4 (December 1965). pp. 1001-1002.

Conway, M.M., Feigert, F.E., *Political Analysis: An Introduction*, (Allen & Bacon, New York, 1972).

Conwell, R.W., *The Childs Construction of Politics*, Melbourne, Australia, Melbourne University Press 1971.

Cortes, Fernando; Przeworski, Adam; and Sprugue John, *Systems Analysis for Social Scientists* (John Wiley and Sons, New York, 1974).

Coser Lewis, A., *Tbe Functions of Social Conflict* (Free Press. Glencoe, Illinois, 1965).

Cosin B.R. (ed), *Educational Structure and Society* (Penguine, Harmondsworth, 1972).

Crick Bernard, *American Science of Politics* (University of California Press, Berkley and Los Angels, 1959).

Colletti Lucion, *From Rousseau to Lenin* (Oxford University Press, Delhi, 1969).

Dahl, Robert A., "Political Theory", *World Politics*, Vol. XI (October 1958), pp. 89-102.

Dahl Robert A. "The Concept of Power", *Behavioural Science* 2, (1957), pp. 201-5.

Dahl Robert A. *Who Governs? Democracy and Power in an American City* (Yale University Press, New Heaven and London, 1961).

Dahrendorf Rolf, *Class and Class Conflict in Industrial Society* (Routledge and Kegan Paul, London, 1957).

Dahrendorf Lalph, *Essays in the Theory of Society*, (Routledge and Kegan Paul, London, 1968).

Dahrendorf Rolf, "Art of Utupia: Toward a Reorientation of Sociological Analysis" *American Journal of Sociology* Vol. LXIV (1958), pp. 115-127.

Das, F.T., "The Dilemma of Criticism in Political Philosophy". *Indian Journal of Political Science*, Vol. 30, (1969), pp. 30-49.

Davies, Morton R and Vaughan, Lewis A., *Models of Political System* (Vikas Publication, New Delhi, 1971).

Dawson R and Prewitt, K. *Political Socialization* (Little Brown and Co., Boston, 1969).

Demareth N. and Peterson R. (eds.), *System Change and Con-*

flict: A Reader in Contemporary Sociological Theories and Debate Over Functionalism (Free Press, New York, 1957).

Dennis, J., Lindberg, L., Crone, D., & Steirbold, R., "Political Socialization to Democratic Orientations in Four Western Systems", *Comparative Political Studies* 1, (1968), pp. 71-101.

Deutsch Karl, W., *The Nerves of Governments Models of Political Communication and Control* (Free Press, New York, 1963).

Deutscher, I., "Word and Deeds: Social Science and Social Policy" *Social Problem*, Vol. 13, (1966), pp. 235-254.

Dobb Maurice, *Theories of Value and Distribution Since Adamsmith* (Cambridge University Press, London, New York, Melbourn, 1977).

Dublin Robert, *Theory Building*, (Free Press, New York, 1969).

Dunning W.A., *A History of Political Theories: Ancient Medieval* (Macmillan, New York, 1902).

Easton David, *A Commitment to Excellence* (Queen's University, Canada, 1976).

Easton David, *A Framework of Political Analysis*, (Prentice-hall, Englewood Cliffs, New Jersey, 1965).

Easton David, "A Re-Assessment of the Concept of Political Support" *British Journal af Political Science* 5, (1975) pp. 435-457.

Easton David, *A Systems Analysis of Political Life*, (Wiley, New York, 1965).

Easton David, *A Theoretical Approach to Authority* (Standford Calif, 1955).

Easton David, "An Approach to the Analysis of Political Systems" in Mosma Stephen V: and Vandersilk Jack R. (eds.) *American Politics: Research and Readings*, (Holt Reinhart and Winston Inc., New York, 1970) pp. 5-18.

Easton David, "Can There be a Science of Human Behaviour?" *University of Chicago Round Table Publication* (October 11, 1953).

Easton David, *Communication Systems and Resources in the Behavioural Sciences* (National Academy of Sciences, Washington, 1967).

Easton David, "Further Comments on Criticism of Systems Analysis' (*Hogaku Kenkyu Journal of Law, Politics and Sociology* 46, (1973), pp. 52-61.

Easton David, "Limits of the Equilibrium Model in Social Research", in Fulan. H, Eldersveld, G.J.M., Janowitz (eds.), *Political Behaviour* (Free Press of Glencol, Illinois, 1956).

Easton David, "Polltical Anthropology" in Siegal B.J. (ed.) *Biennial Review of Anthropology* (Standford University Press, Standford, 1959) pp. 210-62.

Easton David, "Political Science". in Sills David L. (ed.) *International Encyclopedia of Social Sciences* (The Macmillan Company and the Free Press, New York, 1968) Vol. 12, pp. 282-297.

Easton David, "Shifting Images of Social Science and Values" 15, *Antioch Review* (1955), pp. 3-18.

Easton David, "Systems Analysis and Its Classical Critics" *The Political Science Reviewer* 3, (1973) pp. 269-301.

Easton David, "System Analysis in Politics and Its Critics," *Hogaku Kenkyu* 45, (Tokyo, 1972), pp. 46-70.

Easton David, 'The Decline of Modern Political Theory' in Gonld James A. and Thursby Vincent V., (eds.) *Contemporary Political Thought* (Holt Reinhart and Winston Inc., New York, 1969), pp. 307-327.

Easton David, "The Functions of Formal Education in a Political System" *School Review* Vol. 65, (1957), pp. 304-316.

Easton David, "The International Character of National Political Science" *Bulletin, Canadian Political Science Association*, 5, (1976), 1-15.

Easton David, "Theoretical Approaches to Political Support" *Canadian Journal of Political Science*, 9, (1976) pp. 431-448.

Easton David, "The Theoretical Relevance of Political Socialization" *Canadian Journal of Political Science* 1, (1968), pp. 124-146.

Easton David, *The Political System: An Inquiry into the State of Political Science*, (Knofp, New York, 1953).

Easton David, "The Relevance of Biopolitics to Political Theory" in Sanit A. (eds.), *Biology and Politics: Recent Explorations* (Maison des Sciences de l'home et Maison Morton Paris, 1976), pp. 237-247.

Easton David, "Traditional and Behavioural Research in American Political Science", *Administrative Quarterly* 2, (1957), pp. 110-115.

Easton David, (ed.) *Varieties of Political Theory*, (Prenticehall Englewood Cliffs, New Jersey, 1967).

Easton David and Coleman W. "Concept of Support for the Political Community Reconsidered" in S.K. Sharma (ed.), *Dynamics of Development: An International Perspective*, (Concept Publishing Company, 1978).

Easton David and Dennis Jack, *Children in the Political System: Origins of Political Legitimacy* (McGraw Hill Book Company, New York, 1969).

Easton David and Dennis Jack "Politics in the School Curricula" in Morrissett I. and Stevens W.W. Jr. (eds.), *Social Science in the Schools: A Search for Rationale* (Holt Reinhart and Winston, New York, 1971), pp. 72-85.

Easton David and Dennis Jack, "The Child's Acquisition of Regime Norms: Political Efficacy", *American Political Science Review* 61, (1967), pp. 25-38.

Elliott W.Y., *Pragmatic Revolt in Politics* (Macmillan, New York, 1928).

Emery, F.E. (ed.), *Systems Thinking* (Penguin, Harmondsworth, 1969).

Eulan Heinz, *Behavioural Persuasion in Politics* (Valils Feffers and Simons, Bombay, 1963).

Evans Michael, "Notes on David Easton's Model of the Political System" *Journal of Commonwealth Studies*, Vol. 8, (July 1970), pp. 124-129.

Faulkner H.U., *American Political and Social History* (Appleton Century Craft, New York, 1952).

Fay Brian, *Social Theory and Political Practice* (George Allen and Unwin Ltd.. New York, 1975).

Fredrich W. Frey, "Comment: On Issues and Nonissues in the Study of Power" *American Political Science Review* 65, (1971), pp. 1081-1101.

Friedrich C.J., *An Introduction to Political Theory* (Harper and Row, New York, 1967).

Friedrich Robert W., *A Sociology of Sociology* (The Free Press, New York, 1970).

Frohock Fred M., *The Nature of Political Inquiry* (The Dorsey Press, Home Wood Illinois, 1967).

Garner, J.W., *Political Science and Government* (The World Press Calcutta, 1952).

Germino Dante, *Beyond Ideology: The Revival of Political Theory*, (Harper and Row, New York, 1967).

Germino Dante, 'The Revival of Political Theory', *The Journal of Politics*, Vol. 2 (August 1963), pp. 437-460.

Gerth H. H. and Mills C. Wright (eds.) *From Max Weber, Essays in Sociology* (Routledge and Kegan Paul, London, 1948).

Grinker R.R. (ed). *Toward a Unified Theory of Human Behaviour* (Basic Books, New York, 1965).

Greenberg E. S. (ed), *Political Socialization* (Atherton Press, New York, 1970).

Gould James A. Thursby Vincent V. *Contemporary Political Thought Issues in Scope, Value, and Direction* (Holt, Reinhart and Winston Inc., New York, 1969).

Haas Michael and Kariel, Henry S. *Approaches to the Study of Political Science*, (Chandler Publishing Co., California, 1970).

Haddow Hanna, *Political Science in American Colleges Universities from 1636-1900*, Appleton Cantury, New York, 1936).

Handlin, Oscar, *America: A History* (Reinhart and Winston, New York, 1968).

Harsanyi J. C. "Rational Choice Models of Political Behaviour Vs Functional and Conformist Theories" *World Politics*, Vol. 21, No. 4 (July 1969), pp. 513-538.

Heller Herman, "Political Science", in Seligman Edwin R. A.

(ed.) *The Encyclopedia of the Social Sciences* (MacMillan, New York, 1933), Vol. XI, pp.

Hess, R. D. and Easton David, "The Child's Political World" *Midwest Journal of Political Science,* Vol. 4 (1962), pp. 229-246.

Hess R. and Torny J. V. *The Development of Political Attitude in Children*, (Aldine, Chicago, 1967).

Hicks, J. D., 'The Populist Contribution', in Spechan Donald (ed.) *The Making of American History*, (Dryden Press, New York, 1954).

Hirsch, D. Jaros H. and Fleron F. H. "The Melevolent Leader: Political Socialization in an American Subculture", *American Political Science Review* Vol. LXII (1968), pp. 564-575.

Gramsci, Antonis, *Selections from the Prison Note Books of Antonio Gramsci,* ed. and trans. Hoare quintin and Nowell-Smith Geoffrey (International Publishers, New York, 1971).

Harowitza, L. (ed.) *Power Politics and People: The Collected Essays of C. Wright Mills,* (Balantine Books, New York, 1963).

Horowitz Irving L. (ed.) *The New Sociology: Essays in Social Science and Social Theory in Honour of C. Wrights Mills,* (Oxford University Press, New York, 1964).

Horowitz Irving L. (ed.) *The Wise and Abuse of the Social Science,* (E.P. Dutton and Company, New Brunswick, New Jersey, 1971).

Hyman, Herbert H., *Political Socialization* (American Publishing Co., New Delhi, 1972).

Isaak, A. C., *Scope and Methods of Political Science* (Home Wood Dorsey, Home Wood, Illinois, 1967).

James William, Pragmatism (Eurasia Publishing House, New Delhi, 1975).

Jevons W. S., *The Theory of Political Economy* (Cliffton, New Jersey, 1911).

Jones, R.E., *The Functional Analysis of Politics*, (Routledge and Kegan Paul, London, 1967).

Jouvenel B. DE. *The Pure Theory of Politics* (Yale University Press, New Heaven, 1963).

Kaplan, M. A., *Macro Politics: Selected Essays on the Philosophy and Science of Politics*, (Aldims Publishing Company, Chicago, 1969).

Kaplan, M. A., *System and Processes in International Politics* (Wiley, New York, 1953).

Kavanagh Dennis, "Allegiance Among English Children: A Dissent" *British Journal of Political Science*, Vol. 2 (1972), pp. 127-131.

Kellehar G. J. *The Challenge to Systems Analysis* (John Wiley, New Jersey, 1970).

Kress Paul F., 'A Critique of Easton's Systems Analysis' in Gould Jame A. and Thursby Vincent, (eds) *Contemporary Political Thought*, (Holt Reinhart and Winston, Inc., New York, 1919), pp. 211-227.

Kuhn T., *The Structure of Scientific Revolutions* (University of Chicago Press, Chicago, 1970).

Laslett Peter, (ed) *Philosophy, Politics and Society*, first series (Barnes and Noble, New York, 1957).

Lasswell Harold, *Politics Who Gets, What, When, How?* (McGraw Hill, New York, 1936).

Lasswell Harold, *Power and Personality* (Norton, New York, 1948).

Lasswell Harold and Kaplan. A., *Power and Society: A Framework of Political Inquiry*, (Yale University Press, New Heaven, 1950).

Lasswell Harold, *Psychopathology of Politics* (Viking, New York, 1960).

Lasswell Harold, *World Politics and Personal Insecurity* (McGraw Hill, New York, 1953).

Lewis Coser, *The Functions of Social Conflict* (Routledge and Kegan Paul, London, 1956).

Lippman Walter, *A Preface to Politics*, (University of Michigan Press, Ann. Arbor, 1962).

Lippman Walter, *Public Opinion*, (MacMillan, New York, 1947).

Lipset S. M. & Iowenthal L., *Culture and Social Character*, Free Press of Gencoe, New York, 1961).

Loc kwood David, "Some Reflections on the Social System". *British Journal of Sociology*, Vol, VII (June 1956), pp. 134-146.

Lukacs George, *History and Class Consciousness*, Translated by Rowdy Livingstone (Merlin Press, London, 1971).

Mackenzie, W. J. M., *Study of Political Science Today*, (Macmillan, London, 1970).

Mephorson C. B., *Democratic Theory* (Clarendon Press, Oxford 1973).

Mcllwain, C. H., *The Growth of Political Thought in the West: From Greeks T. The Middle Ages* (Macmillan, New York, 1932).

McCoy C. A. and Playford, J. (eds.) *Apolitical Politics* (Thomas and Govrell, New York, 1967).

Marsh David, "Political Socialization: The Implicit Assumptions questioned" *British Journal of Political Science*, Vol. 1 (1971), pp. 450-58.

Martin dale. Don (ed) *Functionalism in the Social Sciences: The Strength and Limits of Functionalism in Anthropology, Economics, Political Science, and Sociology*, (The American Academy of Political and Social Science, Philadelphia, 1965).

Marx Karl, *A Contribution to the Critique of Political Economy*. (Progress Publishers, Moscow, 1970).

Marx K. *German Ideology* (Lawrence and Wishart, London, 1965).

Meehan Eugene, *Contemporary Political Thought* (Dorsey Press, Home Wood Illinois, 1967).

Meek Ronald, E. *Studies in the Labour Theory of Value* (Monthly Review Press, New York and London, 1956).

Menzies Ken. *Talcott Parsons and Social Image of Man* (Routledge and Kegan Paul, London, 1976).

Merriam, Charles E., Barnes, Hany E., (ed.) *A History of Political Theories in Recent Times : Essay in Contemporary Development in Political Theory* (McMillan, New York, 1924).

Merriam, Charles E., *New Aspects of Politics* (University of Chicago, Chicago, 1925).

Merriam, Charles E., *Political Power : Its Composition and* Incidence (McGraw Hill, New York, 1934).

Merriam Charles E., *Systematic Politics* (University of Chicago Press, Chicago, 1945).

Merriam Charles E., *The Role of Politics in Social Change* (New York University Press, New York, 1936).

Miliband Ralph, *Marxism and Politics* (Oxford University Press, Oxford, 1977).

Mills C.W., *The Sociological Imagination* (Oxford University Press, London, 1959).

Mitchell W.C., "Politics as the Allocation of Values : A Critique", *Ethics* Vol. LXXI (Jan 1963), No. 2, pp. 79-87.

Mitchel W.C., *The American Policy*, (Free Press of Glencoe, New York, 1962).

Moore Barrington, *Political Power and Social Theory*. (Harvard University Press, Cambridge Mass. 1958).

Morgenthan, Hans. J. *Politics Among Nations* (Nopf, New York, 1948).

Munro W.B., "Physics and Politics : An Old Analogy Reviewed" Vol. XXII, No. 1, (February 1928), pp. 1-11.

Nibset, R.A., *Social Changes and History* : *Aspects of Western Theory of Development* (Oxford University Press, New York, 1959).

Novack, George, *Pragmatism Versus Marxism*, (Pathfinders Press, New York, 1975).

Nye, R.B., and Morpurgo, J.E., *A History of the United States* : *The Growth of the U.S.A.* (Penguine Press, Hammands Worth, 1965).

Pammet Jon H., "The Development of Political Orientations" *Canadian Journal of Political Science*, Vol. IV (1971), pp. 132-141.

Parrington Vernon Louis, *Main Currents in American Thought* (Harcourt, New York, 1958).

Parsons Talcott, *The Social System* (Macmillan Company, New York, 1951).

Phillips D.C., *Halistic Thought in Social Sciences* (Macmillan New York, 1977).

Popper Karl R., *The Poverty of Historicism* (Routledge and Kegan Paul, London, 1957).

Radcliff-Brown, A.R., *A Natural Science of Society* (Free Press, New York, 1957).

Ranney, Austin, (ed.) *Essays on the Behavioural Study of Politics* (University of Illinois Press, Urbana, 1962).

Ranney Austin, *The Governing Man* (Holt, New York, 1966).

Reed Thomas H., and Reed Doris D., *Preparing College Men and Women for Politics*, (The Law Centre of New York University, New York, 1952).

Reimer Neal, *The Revival of Democratic Theory*, (Appleton-Century-Crofts, New York, 1962).

Rex J., *Key Problems in Sociological Theory*, (Routledge and Kegan Paul, London, 1961).

Rice Stuart A., *Quantitative Methods in Politics*, (Knopf, New York, 1928).

Robson, James, A., "Decision Making, Political Aspects", in *The International Encyclopedia of Social Sciences*, (The Macmillan Company and the Free Press, New York, 1968), Vol 4, pp. 55-56.

Robson William A., *The University Teaching of Social Sciences : Political Science* (UNESCO, Paris, 1954).

Roseman Cysil, Mayo Charles G., and Collinge F.B., *Dimensions of Political Analysis* (Prenticehall Englewood Cliffs New Jersey, 1965).

Roszak Theodore (ed.) *The Dissenting Academy* (Pantheon Books, New York, 1968).

Russet C.E., *Concept of Equilibrium in American Social Thought* (Yale University Press, New York, 1965).

Ryan A., *The Philosophy of the Social Sciences*, (Pantheon Books, New York, 1970).

Sandor Holebsky, *Mass Society and Political Conflict*, (Cambridge University Press, Cambridge, London 1976).

Singh Randhir, *Reason Revolution and Political Theory*, (People's Publishing House, New York, 1976).

Somit A. and Tananhaus J., *The Development of American Political Science : From Burgess to Behaviouralism*, (Ally and Becon, Boston, 1967).

Spragen T.A., *The Dilemma of Contemporary Political Theory : Toward a Post-Behavioural Science of Politics* (Dunellen, New York, 1973).

Sommerhoff G., *Analytical Biology* (Oxford University Press, London, 1950).

Stephens J., "The logic of Functional and Systems Analysis in Political Science", *Midwest Journal of Political Science*, Vol. 13 (1971), pp. 367-399.

Stogdill, R.M., *The Progress of Model Building in the Behavioural Sciences* (Ohio State University Press, Columbia, 1970).

Streeten Paul (ed.) *Values in Social Theory* : A Selection of Essays on Methodology (Routledge and Kegan Paul, London, 1958).

Solapool Ithiel de, (ed) *Contemporary Political Science : Toward Empirical Theory* (McGraw Hill Book Company, New York, 1967).

Sorokin Pitrim, A., *Contemporary Sociological Theories*, (Harper, New York, 1928).

Sorokin Pitrim, A., *Society Culture and Personality*, (Harper, New York, 1947).

Thorson Thomas Ladon, *Biopolitics* (Holt Reinhart and Winston Inc., New York, 1970).

Timasheff Nicholas S., *Sociological Theory* (Random House, New York, 1965).

Truman D.B., *The Governmental Process* (Knopf, New York, 1951).

Valliancart Pauline Mari, "Stability of Children's Survey Responses", *Public Opinion Quarterly*, Vol. XXXVII (1969), pp. 373-387.

Vandyke Vernon, *Political Science : A Philosophical Analysis*, (Standford University Press, Standford, California, 1960).

Varney, D.V., *The Analysis of Political Systems* (Routledge and Kegan Paul, London, 1959).

Verma, S.P., *Modern Political Theory* (Vaikash Publishing House, New Delhi, 1975).

Waldo Dwight, "Political Science : Tradition, Discipline, Profession, Science, Enterprise", in Greenstein Fred 9., and Polsby Nelson W., (eds) *Handbook of Political Science*, Vol. I. (Addison-Wesley Publishing Co., Reading, 1975).

Wallas Graham, *Human Nature in Politics*, (Orient and Longman, Bombay, 1948).

Watkings F.M., *The State As a Concept of Political Science*, (Harper, New York, 1934).

Weber Max, *The Theory of Social and Economic Organization*, (The Free Press, Illinois, 1964).

Weinbarg J.R., "On Sabine's Philosophy of Value" in Konowitz Milton R. and Murphy Arthur E., (eds) *Essays in Poli-*

tical Theory (Kennikat Press, Port Washington, New York, 1948).

White, Morton, *Social Thought in America* (Beacon Press, Boston 1957).

Wicker A.W., "Attitudes Versus Actions : The Relationship of Verbal and Overt Behavioural Responses to Attitudes Objects", *Journal of Social Issues* Vol. 25 (1969) pp. 41-78.

Winstein, M.A., *Philosophy Theory and Method in Contemporary Political Thought*. (Scott Froesman Glenview, Illinois, 1971).

Wiseman, H.V., *Political Systems : Some Sociological Approaches* (Routledge and Kegan Paul, London, 1966).

Wiseman, H.V., *Politics the Master Science* (Routledge and Kegan Paul, London, 1969).

Welstergaard J. and Resler H., *State in the Capitalists Society*, (Penguine Harmondsworth, 1976).

Young, O.R., "A Survey of General Systems Theory", *General Systems*, Vol. 9 (1964), pp. 61-80.

Young, O.R., Systems of Political Science, (Prentice Hall, Englewood Cliffs, Inc., New Jersey, 1968).

Young, R., *Approaches to the Study of Politics* (North Western University Press, Evanston, Illinois, 1958).

Index

OUR OUTSTANDING PUBLICATIONS

Ahangar, Mohd. Altaf Hussain	Customary Succession Among Muslims.	1986	175.00
Amir Hussain, IAS	A Tribe in Turmoil : Socio-Economic Study of Jammu Gujars of Uttar Pradesh.	1986	150.00
Anderson, G.	The expanision of British India	1987	150.00
Balasubamanian, M.	Nehru : A Study in Secularism.	1980	45.00
Banerjea, Pramathanath	Public Administration in Ancient India.	1985	125.00
Barman, Kiran	Public Debt Management in India.	1986	150.00
Baruah, A.K.	Systems Analysis in Political Science : A Marxit Critique of David Easton.	1987	125.00
Bawa, Noorjahan	People's Participation Development Adm. in India.	1985	125.00
Bayti, Jamnalal	Readings in Education.	1986	150.00
Bayti, Jamnalal	Problems of Education in the third world.	1987	150.00
Bhattacharjee, Debasish	Bureacracy and Development in Meghalaya.	1986	150.00
Bhattacharya, Mohit	Management of Urban Government in India.	1976	50.00
Bhattacharya, Mohit	Bureaucracy and development Administration.	1979	50.00
Bhargava, P.K.	Essays on Indian Economic Planning.	1985	90.00
Bhargava, P.K.	Some Aspects of Indian Public Finances.	1984	125.00
Bhaskara Rao, V.	General elections in India (Some Issues of Eighth Lok Sabha Elections)	1987	150.00

Kaushik, S.N.	Pakistan under Bhutto's Leadership.	1985	175.00
Kamble, N.D.	Bonded Labour in India.	1982	60.00
Kamble, N.D.	Migrants in Indian Metropolis.	1982	75.00
Kedia, Kusum Lata	Local Finance in an Indian State : Municipal Finance of Varanasi Division Since 1951-	1986	200.00
Khan, Mumtaz Ali	Scheduled Caste and their Status in India.	1980	75.00
Khan, Mumtaz Ali	Status of Rural Women in India.	1982	75.00
Khan, Mumtaz Ali	Social Legislation and the Rural Poor.	1981	50.00
Khan, Mumtaz Ali	Muslims in the Process of Rural Development in India	1984	150.00
Krishnakumari, N.S.	Status of Single Women in India.	1987	150.00
Mandal, B.B.	Tribals at the Polls : A Study of Khunti in Chotanagpur-	1986	90.00
Madan, J.C.	Indian Police.	1980	110.00
Mahendra Singh	Indo-U.S. Relations : A Political Study.	1985	75.00
Malik, Inder Lal	Dalai Lamas of Tibet.	1984	90.00
Menon, M. Indu	Status of Muslim Women in India.	1981	50.00
Mishra, Upendra	Caste and Politics in India.	1986	225.00
Mishra, S.N. and Kushal Sharma	Problems and Prospects of Rural Development in India.	1983	80.00
Mohan, N. Shantha	Status of Nurses in India.	1985	60.00
Mukarji, Nirmal and Banerjee, Ashis	Democracy Federalism and the feature of India's unity.	1987	60.00
Padhi, A.P. and Mishra, Sommanath	State Administration in India.	1987	300.00

Pal, J.J.	Jinnah and the creation of Pakistan.	1985	75.00
Paliwal, M.R.	Social Change and Education.	1984	175.00
Paliwal, M.R.	The Teacher Education on the Move : Today and Tomorrow.	1985	225.00
Paliwal, M.R.	Differential Effectiveness of Micro-learning.	1984	50.00
Pai Panandiker, V.A. and Arun Sud.	Changing Political Representation in India.	1983	65.00
Pai Panandikar, V.A. and Ajay K. Mehra	People's Participation in Family Planning.	1987	160.00
Pai Panandiker, V.A., R.N. Bisnnoi and O.P. Sharma	Organisational Policy for Family Planning.	1983	125.00
Pai Panandiker, V.A. and P.N. Chaudhuri	Demographic Transition in Goa and its Policy Implications.	1983	40.00
Panda, Basudev	Indian Bureaucracy : An Inside Story.	1978	60.00
Pandey, K.K.	Rural Development in India : Continuity and Change.	1986	125.00
Pandey, Jawaharlal	State Politics in India.	1982	90.00
Pandey, S.K. Sharma	Deway Decimal Classification for Indology.	1979	200.00
Partap Singh	Urban Government in India.	1978	45.00
Pillai, G. Narayana	Social Background of Political Leadership in India.	1983	90.00
Rai, Haridwar and S.P. Singh	Current Ideas and Issues in Indian Administration.	1979	70.00
Rajgopal, P.R.	Communal Violence in India.	1987	140.00
Rajjan Lal and Kidwai, Nasira	Practical Cataloguing Procedure (Hindi).	1980	95.00
Rastogi, P.N.	India 1981-86 : A forecaste on Econcmic, Political and Social Developments.	1982	50 .00

Redy, P. Ranjani	The Role of Dominant Caste in Indian Politics.	1987	150.00
Rawlinson, H.G.	Shivaji the Maratha : his Life and Time.	1984	75.00
Rawlinson, H.G.	Indian Historical studies.	1987	200.00
Ray, B. Datta	The Emergence and Role of Middle Class in North East India.	1983	100.00
Ray, B. Datta	The Pattern and Problems of Population in North-East India.	1986	250.00
Rita Khanna	Agricultural Mechanisation and Social Change in India.	1983	125.00
Roy, R.C., IAS	State Public Enterprise in India.	1986	200.00
Saksena, H.S.	Safeguards for Scheduled Castes and Tribes : Founding Father's View.	1981	200.00
Seshadri, K.	Studies in the problems of the third world.	1986	175.00
Seshadri, K.	Studies in Indian Polity.	1986	150.00
Sharma, O.P.	Great Men of India.	1987	150.00
Sharma, P.D.	Police and Criminal Justice Administration in India.	1985	125.00
Sharma, P.D.	Police, Polity and People in India.	1981	125.00
Sharma, R.N. & Bakshi Santosh	Tribes and Tribal Development : Select Bibliography.	1984	250.00
Sharma, T.R.	New Challenges in Indian Politics.	1986	175.00
Shrivastava, M.P.	Problems of Accountability of Public Enterprise in India.	1986	225.00
Sikka, R.P.	The Civil Service in India.	1984	150.00
Sinha, R.P.	Social Dimensions of Trade Unionism in India.	1986	90.00
Singh, K.P.	Tribal Development in India.	1987	150.00

ingh, L.P.	Sardar Patel and Indian Administration	1987	25.00
Singh, L.P.	Electoral Reform.	1986	95.00
Singh, L.P.	India's Foreign Policy	1980	55.00
Singh, S.P.	Perspectives in Indian Politics and Administration.	1981	60.00
Singh, S.S.	Administration of Natural Justice in India.	1986	250.00
Singh, S.S. and S. Sundram	Emerging Harijan Elite : A Study of their Identity.	1987	125.00
Sundeep Khanna, IAS	Civil Administration in India.	1983	60.00
Trivedi, B.V.	Prison Administration in India : Model Prison Programme.	1987	125.00
Verma, S.P.	Indian Parliamentarians : A Study of the Socio-Political Background.	1986	90.00
Vijay Kumar	India and Srilanka-China Relations 1948-84.	1986	125.00
Wishwakarama, R.K.	Urban and Regional Planning Policy in India.	1981	75.00

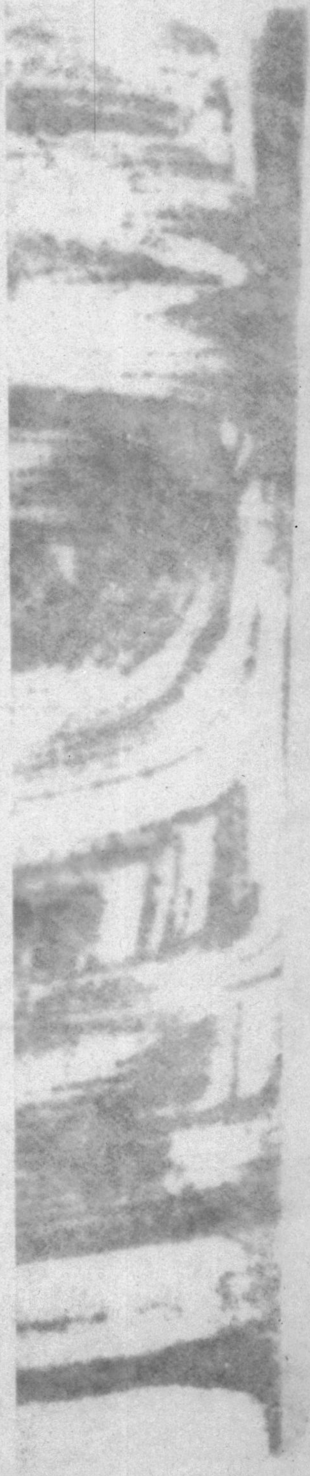